Death From Illicit Brew

Illicit brew killed my father.

PETER N. MUYA

Death From Illicit Brew

Peter N Muya

Published by Peter N Muya, 2024.

Death From Illicit Brew

PETER N. MUYA

Published by Bishop Peter N. Muya

First edition. July 2024.

Second edition. May 2025

Copyright © 2025 Peter N Muya.

ISBN 9798227049827

For information contact Bishop Peter Muya via Email: muyabishop@gmail.com or via phone: +254724805868/+254798649468

Edited by Peter Hinga Kiago. Email: quibpet3r@gmail.com phone: +254706488565

DEDICATION

I DEDICATE THIS WORK to all youths who are struggling to be freed from alcoholic slavery.

CHAPTER ONE
ESCAPE FROM DEATH

FOUR OF EVERY 100 DEATHS in Kenya are linked to illicit brew or drug abuse. Five victims died and five others died before reaching a hospital after drinking toxic illicit brew in a local den in Hodi Hodi Estate in Bahati of Nakuru County. Early December 2021 in Njoro town, eight people died after drinking illicit brew in an informal settlement.

The victims started showing several symptoms, such as vomiting, frothing, blindness, and severe stomach ache. Some victims died in a local hospital while the others died in level five Hospital in Nakuru city. Residents were shocked after losing their loved ones from this poisonous liquor.

Illicit brew was rampant in the villages and estates; it is very dangerous to the community and especially to our youths. As a pastor I would kindly call on the government to eradicate all illicit brews in our country. The police should arrest the culprits and sue them for these evil crimes.

In the Kiambogo village, an old man was seeking happiness after drinking toxic liquor and unfortunately he died because of it, leaving his family in trouble. "Who killed my husband?" the victim's wife wondered in disbelief. When I attended the burial of this poor victim, I thanked God that I was completely transformed before I could have met the same fate. I will never forget the new experience of transformation when I surrendered my life to Jesus. I became a new creature.

I escaped death. I was raised in a toxic atmosphere. My parents were perpetual drunkards. It seemed that the devil had planned to drive me to hell since the beginning. I had a fatal accident when I was high on drugs. My life was miserable as a drug addict. The police were always searching me for drug-related crimes.

I was bound with chains that I could not see. My life was torn. My trousers and shirt were torn. I was wearing worn-out shoes. I could not bathe for days because of hopelessness and depression. I was angry about my life and angry with everybody. I thought everybody was against me. My family and relatives thought something must have been wrong with me. I could not concentrate or make even simple decisions in life. I couldn't plan on what to eat or wear each day.

It was a shattering experience suffering from such depression. Sleeping was sometimes very difficult at night. Whenever I'd wake up in the morning, I'd felt a black cloud hovering over my life, and I was disappointed. I thought about My sister Jane who was always under medication from depression. My life was full of agony and misery. The fear of ending up in a mental hospital like my sister disturbed me. Because of drug abuse, my mind was not functioning properly.

My family tried to help, but I slipped and ploughed back into addictions. Stress was a constant disorder in my life. The gravity of my predicament made me think of committing suicide. Sometimes friends came to visit me and found me laughing without cause. Laughing, but living in pain. I could not marry because no girl would accept me in that condition. I was suffering from joblessness and failures in life. I could not fulfill any of my expectations.

DEATH FROM ILLICIT BREW

Today, I am seeing alcoholics and drug abusers suffering like I was. Victims are consuming illicit brews that are mixed with a very poisonous chemical substance called "ethanol" that interferes with the organs in the body, causing many deaths. Victims are complaining of regular headaches, ulcers, nausea, heart problems, and high blood pressure. There are many ills that are linked to the addiction of this illicit brew in the market.

Families are always demonstrating to show the world dangers caused by abusing these illegal substances. Thousands of wives are complaining that their husbands are impotent in bed. Their manhood was destroyed by these illicit brews. Millions of our youth are drowning into the evil sea of drug addiction and alcoholism. As a result, criminal activity is increasing in our society. Victims are suffering from the damaging consequences of addictions.

Drug and substance abuse gives the abusers an artificial source of well-being and causes them to suffer more when they try to withdraw. Our youth are suffering physically, emotionally, and mentally. The addicts call drugs "herbs." God has given every human being the freedom to choose. You can choose life or death, blessings or curses (Deuteronomy 30:19). And many youths have chosen death.

This is why I'm helping the youth today to choose life. I'm warning the youth by telling them that there is "death in the pot of the illicit brew." I have volunteered to rescue the youth from drug addiction.

I warn the youth to not allow themselves to become addicted to smoking cigarettes because the poisonous chemicals within them like nicotine, carbon monoxide, and others will get into their heart by passing through their blood throughout the whole body. They'll start staggering, trembling with imbalance because of muscular paralysis. And once these chemicals pass through their lungs, they can develop lung, liver, or kidney cancers. Stomach ulcers can also be caused, which could lead to death.

My message to everybody is that there is death in the pot of the illicit brew. Look for example at the people of Central Rift Valley. They are blessed with very productive land, but instead of making use of their land, they are involving themselves with alcoholism and drug abuse. We have seen thousands of victims becoming blind, and others becoming impotent. Others develop vision problems. And a lot of domestic violence rises in homes.

I'm telling the youth this story. One day in Israel, people there were experiencing famine in the land. One of the sons of the prophet went out in the open field and brought herbs and wild vine. After cooking, the hungry were served, but while they were eating, they all cried, saying to the prophet, Elisha, "O' man of God, there is death in the pot" (2 Kings 4:38–41). When the prophet prayed after that, he destroyed the spirit of death in the pot.

This is why today, as a former addict but now a servant of God, I am declaring that there is death in the pot! Stop abusing the "herbs," or wild vine. God is against the herbs and wild vine because they cause death.

Drug addicts and alcoholics invite poverty into their homes. The Bible warns, "Woe to those who rise early in the morning so that they may run after strong drinks and those who tarry late into the evening as wine inflames them" (Isaiah

5:11*)*. The Bible warns the breweries that make different brands of liquor, "Woe to he who makes his neighbors drink. You pour out your wrath and make them drunk in order to gaze at their nakedness" (Habakkuk 2:15). The Bible says that "For the drunkard and the glutton shall come to poverty and drowsiness shall clothe a man with rags" (Proverbs 23-21).

One second-generation liquor brand is called "sting." Why? Because the Bible says it "stings like an adder and bites like a serpent" (Proverbs 23:29). Another brand is called "fighter" because it fights the victims physically, mentally, emotionally, and financially.

"Wine is a mocker, a strong drink is a brawler, and whoever is led astray by such a drink is not wise" (Proverbs 20:1*)*. Are you a victim who is being led astray by wine? Call Jesus Christ today into your heart, and you will be totally saved and transformed.

I Escaped From Death

Drugs could make me forget my problems, but only for a moment. I wanted to end my life. I felt a feeling that the dead were happier than I was. I wanted to die and meet the happy guys in hell. I could not sleep at night when I thought about my problems and misfortunes. I felt as if nobody loved me or understood me. I felt as if everybody was against me. I was experiencing hell, and I felt that God had abandoned me. The world treated me with injustice. I was tired of living in this world of unrest. I thought that one day I would rest in my soul.

In desperation and hopelessness, I attempted suicide, but before I perished in drug addiction, God's plan of deliverance prevailed. I realized that I was lost in sins and that I was heading for the deepest depths of hell. I willingly surrendered my miserable life to Jesus. I was delivered and transformed. I escaped hell by a whisker.

I was first born of my mother, and she nurtured me as a baby and brought me up. But later in Kiambogo, twenty-something years afterwards, I was born again of the Spirit. I received a new life that is different from the natural life. I obtained a life that is everlasting and of peace. It was not a self-planned experience; it was not emotional, yet it affected me all over mentally, spiritually, and physically.

I praised the LORD that night with joy, which was unexplainable. It was not until later when I learnt many wonderful lessons on the subject of this new birth. I knew that something thrilling had happened in my life. The next thing I knew was that I was awake and immediately felt like my confused mind was healed. I also remembered that Jesus had told me to trust in Him. He promised me that He would lead me until I saw His face again. Truly Jesus is real. "His name is Love." I proved it.

Early the next morning, I woke up and went to tell my brother, David, about my new experience. I began by telling him everything that had happened since I saw Jesus. I told him the whole story, and he was amazed by it, anxiously listening because he had passed through the same experience one year ago. David took his bible and quoted to me this scripture: "Therefore, if any man be in Christ, he is a new creature. Old things are passed away. Behold. All things became new" (1 Corinthians 5:17).

Before I had experienced this new birth, I was not happy. I was always striving to attain something worthy for my future. But upon this new birth, everything in my life was laid before my Lord, Jesus, who cares for me more than I do. Since then, success seemed to be the most important thing in my life. I became a successful soul-winner in my village, and this brought me real joy, a peace of mind, and a new assurance for my future.

My life was completely covered eternally in Jesus Christ. "For ye are dead, and your life is hiding with Christ in God" (Colossians 3:3). I found myself being changed by this supernatural power into a Christ-loving, Bible-reading, praying Christian. It was a miracle! No works of mine were required. The moment I believed so, it happened—Hallelujah! "For by grace are ye saved through faith, and that not of yourselves. It is the gift of God" (Ephesians 2:8).

As for my old pals, they were not satisfied with my changed life. They considered me as a stricken deer or a buffalo that had left the herd. I was a different creature before them. I was in a different world where I freely talked about God in every opportunity and tried to win souls for Christ in every spare moment. I often sang hymns in church and at home instead of the popular pop music, which I used to sing before. This proved that I had been transformed into a completely different person in my old friends' eyes. I knew how the change took place, but I surely could not have made them understand until they experienced it themselves.

As for me, my inner eyes had been widely opened to the realities of the spiritual world. I realized that the Bible was really the words of God that, when obeyed, can cause miracles to happen. I saw that the Bible was full of wonderful promises for me. It also revealed to me tenderness and nearness of God in Christ, which satisfied my heart's longing and showed me that the infinite God is the creator of the world who took our nature upon Him so that we might be one in His great love.

I believe in the Bible because it reveals a religion adapted to all classes and races in the world. The Bible states clearly that all people are the same worldwide. I believe that it is an intellectual suicide knowing all this and not believing it. Perhaps one of my strongest reasons for believing the Bible is that it revealed to me a spiritual diagnosis for my condition. It showed me clearly what I was by nature—one who was lost in sin and alienated from the life that is in God. I found it to be a consistent and wonderful revelation of the character of God, who removed me from my natural imaginations.

As faith continued to reveal God to me, I was able to go without question whenever He led me. I always put His assertions and commands above every seeming probability in life, and I entertained cherished convictions. I could trust Him through whatever would happen in the course of believing Him. I'm always prepared to stand alone when declaring Him to be the truth and the way and life worldwide.

"The LORD is my light and my salvation; whom shall I fear? The Lord is the strength of my life; of whom shall I be afraid?" (Psalms 27:1). Had He not told me personally, "Fear not, I'm JESUS?" I shall never forget this phenomenon in myself.

I was a survivor in search of a new beginning. I offered a vivid account of how I met Jesus and how I escaped from death. I dubbed my powerful testimony "Escape From Death." Answers for my life emerged, in addition to fulfilling and transforming power. I told my friends, family, and neighbors that resolutely trusting in Jesus would change their behavior and their lives as well. After my absolution, I started an ongoing campaign to rescue young people from evil behaviors like drug abuse, alcoholism, and fornication, and help them to escape hell and premature death as well.

CHAPTER TWO
ILLICIT BREW KILLED MY FATHER

ON A HOT, DUSTY, DRY day over thirty years ago, God appeared in our poverty-stricken family. We, the "Muyas," were born and brought up in a family of five girls and four boys.

My brother, David Muya, was the first member of our family to accept Jesus Christ as his personal savior in 1977. One year later, after observing my brother's changed life, I also accepted Jesus Christ as my personal savior.

We attended Full Gospel Church in the Kiambogo Village in Elementaita. We continued to pray to God to help our family. In 1979, God miraculously answered our prayers. My brother was employed as a primary school teacher by the teacher's service commission. He was posted in the Molo division.

After I grew up spiritually in the village church, I became a very effective soul-winner. I was volunteering to go out with the pastor and the evangelical team in the open-air meeting every evening. I was winning souls for Christ.

Although finances are essential to any worker in the ministry, this was not my goal in life. I was always out to win souls for Christ without compromise and without expecting any money. God was meeting my needs according to His riches and glory. Through my moving testimony, the Spirit of God touched my sister, Teresiah Muya, and she accepted Jesus Christ as her personal savior in 1980.

At Home

One morning, I woke up and felt pressed in my spirit to speak about the love of God to my family around the fire. I sat next to my younger sisters. They were all staring at the pot of fermented porridge in the fire. Soon, Mother removed the pot out of the fire and begun to stir it with a calabash to cool it. Everyone was silently waiting for his or her share of it.

Suddenly, Father broke the silence. "Nowadays, the sun is becoming so hot that even such porridge cannot quench my thirst. Only a bottle of chang'aa (local liquor) can do me the proper cure." Father had said this while looking at Mother to propose his motion.

Mother looked at my father in the face as she was filling his cup with a gingerly and wobbling stream of porridge. She responded, "In fact, we shall bury you soon if you keep on drinking this dangerous liquor. You don't make me happy by taking chang'aa."

Everyone became silent again. "Jesus loves you all," I said to break the silence. "Without Jesus, man will never be satisfied in this world. Jesus is the only drink that can quench the thirst in every man of whatever race or situation in life." In response, Father looked at me as though the words were tearing the inside of his being, and he went to drink chang'aa without saying a word.

At home, I usually sat beside the fire reading the Bible to my younger sisters and talking about heaven at every given opportunity. Let me say that this was an astonishing spectacle to my family, who were non-believers, and mostly to my father, Muya, who was sullen much of the time.

My father was a short, notorious village elder with crooked ways of life. He lived recklessly and drank far too much. He would not leave the pub until late at night. In fact, it is not an exaggeration to say that he did not wear one pair of shoes in his life; he was drinking all day long. His dear wife, Veronica Nyambura, my mother, had long deserted the evil ways and embraced religion.

Mother was plump and liked tea a lot. Her bitter moment came when she learned that her loving husband was in the hands of the police, having been arrested for being drunk and disorderly. It seemed fateful that my father was a failure in life, yet it must be said that my mother was kind and obeyed him as her husband. She could be heard rebuking neighbors and relatives who tried to create curiosity and family wrangle by alleging that her husband was a perpetual drunkard.

Since the change in me had been so sudden for my family to conceive, they thought that I was somehow crazy. Not only were they disturbed about me, but they were also frightened by the probability of having a nut in the family. Despite all my reasoning from the Bible and showing them the great advantage of knowing Christ as our savior, they still remained aloof of my convictions. I am glad to say that my testimony has reversed the corrupt ways of life in my family.

Praise the Lord! I was sure that my mother and her other children who were not saved would soon grasp the impact of this faith in Jesus Christ. Also, I believed that before the second coming of Christ, everybody in my family would experience this beautiful love of Jesus. I also praised the Lord that even my father, who at first was a bitter opposer of my testimony, would ask for a Bible to read in his spare time. But unfortunately, he died suddenly, having no hope of receiving eternal life. When preachers and Christians persuaded him to repent, he always promised that he would "repent tomorrow." But alas, that "tomorrow" never came!

My father was an alcoholic, and although alcohol had destroyed his life, he could not stop drinking. He could not believe in God even in the day when he was suffering and in severe pain in his bed at Kenyatta National Hospital, where he was admitted with acute kidney failure. The doctors tried hard to save his life but to no avail. So, they discharged him, and after a week, he peacefully died at home.

My father was gone, never to be seen again in this world. He died a miserable sinner. Mother had left him beside the fire warming and listening to the radio as she went to bed that night, but she was surprised to wake up and see him dead on the ground. She gazed with disbelief at the dark-brown coat that he had been wearing. That night my younger sister had been sleeping in the opposite room when Mother touched her with a trembling hand and woke her up. They put the body on his bed.

My brother and I were sleeping in a separate house some meters away from my father's house. But when the news of my father's death reached us, I fell into depression. Seeking help and comfort, I consulted my elder brother, who listened gravely as I poured out my grief on his shoulder.

My God spoke to me through the Spirit. "It is time," He said, "for you to turn away from earthly griefs and seek eternal blessing." The Spirit convinced me of eternal peace within Jesus Christ. That peace was beyond my understanding. However, that perfect peace is valued in my life above all worldly things.

DEATH FROM ILLICIT BREW

The real shock gripped my heart when I looked at my father's dead body, with its smooth black face. He died suddenly before the day he called "tomorrow." I looked again at my father. He was wrapped in a blanket in his bed. "Is this the same father who had been so full of laughter last night after we had a cup of tea together before going to bed?" I asked as I shuddered inwardly. I said in my heart, "No. This is just a cold dead shell I'm looking at with a dull face."

My family then joined me in loud mourning. "But, where is that living personality that had evidently vacated that bruised body?" I shuddered again at the answer to that question. Never in life could this awful moment have been so real to me as I looked down at my father's dead body. He was at the dead's party, and I was fully convinced that sooner or later, everybody would be waiting for this awful call whether they liked it or not. All of my brothers, sisters, and relatives were called in. My father's family was also summoned.

Amos was my father's youngest brother, the only member of his family close to us. Both were born in a family of five in the Ngecha Village in Limuru. They all went to school together, and later my father left school and announced to his tearful parents that he was going to Rift Valley Province at Nakuru Town to seek employment. In 1950, my father got married to my mother as a second wife. The following year they were blessed with a beautiful daughter.

Amos, my father's brother, traveled periodically to Nakuru with presents of cassava to make my father return home, according to traditional belief. But, Father just couldn't. He chose to live in the Rift Valley until his death.

Before the family and the relatives came, my sister, Wanjiru, who is a devoted Christian, gave us moral support. She brought a group of pious youth who performed a perfect work of praising the Lord. Each night they brought the drums, and my sister selected the most beautiful chorus, which touched everybody in my family. She turned our mourning into joy. In our family, we are taught to praise God for all things, just as the Bible implores Christians to rejoice always.

After three days of grief, everybody in my extended family was present in our home ready to escort their departed kin to his final resting place. I imagined Dad teetering on the brink of eternal ruin — "Poor Dad," I spoke inwardly as I paid my final respects to him. "I wish you knew that your death was so near and that God is real. You would have confessed your sins, but now it is too late. Goodbye, Dad!"

Jesus sustained me in His power to overcome this moment of grief. If I had been lying there like my father, I knew for sure I would have gone straight to heaven. However, my father's testimony was so ugly. He lived as a drunkard and eventually died a drunkard. What fool could not read the Bible and then know the fate of my father at once? No amount of sprinkled water nor our petitions could have changed his destiny. Only Him alone would have been able to answer for Father's deeds when judgment day would come.

This event changed everything in my family. However, God assured me that my life was hidden in Jesus Christ, so there was no need for me to fear death. And I heard a voice from Heaven saying unto me, "Blessed are the dead who die in the Lord from henceforth: Yea, saith the Spirit that they may rest from their labors; and their work do follow them" (Revelation 14:13).

Jesus is my savior, and He also provides everything in my life. He is above my joy. "His name is love...Precious in the sight of the Lord is the death of his saints" (Psa. 116:15). My dear friend, let me say that I can cover sheets and sheets of paper, but yet I cannot write even half of what I feel. No human can explain

CHAPTER THREE
DEATH FROM ILLICIT BREW.

YES. WE ARE INDEED living in the most dangerous days when lawlessness, immorality, inflation, and corruption are running very fast; when every kind of evil is displayed in every nation so plainly.

Crime and violence are increasing due to the fact that our prisons are overflowing with condemned criminals and suspects. On the other hand, the horrifying reports of the rapid spreading of fatal diseases like HIV/AIDS and cancer are increasing in every nation on Earth.

In Kenya today, drugs and substances are emerging as a serious security challenge. This is due to our country being located along the Eastern African coast. Kenya is serving as a transit point for narcotic drugs from abroad. That's why on our coastline and in other parts of our country we have thousands of hopeless drug abusers sitting helplessly in the shadow of death, not knowing which way to turn to find total healing and deliverance from addictions.

As a former drug addict and a consumer of illicit brew in Ghettos, God has given me a ministry to rescue drug addicts and drunkards before they perish. Through my ministry, I am warning the abusers that there is death in bottle of illicit brew. We hear bad news in the media of drug addicts and alcoholics raping, committing suicide, killing their wives and children, and dying of the health effects after abusing drugs or alcohol.

In the Bible, you can read the thrilling story about the sons of the prophets who, during a famine, went in the field to gather herbs and ended up finding a wild vine. They brought it back home so that it could be cooked and served as a meal to give to people. As they ate, they sensed death in the pot. They cried to the prophet, Elisha, saying, "O' man of God, there is death in the pot." When the prophet of God prayed and rebuked the spirit of death, there was no longer any harm lurking in the pot's content (2 Kings 4:38–41).

Drug addicts call some drugs the "herb or the stem." That's why I am warning them that there is "death in the pot." In the villages, the illicit brewers use large pots to put the poisonous substances in and then sell to their customers. I am warning the brewers and the customers that there is death in the pot of the illicit brew pot.

In the central province, from the beginning, the Kikuyus used to drink their traditional brew known as "Muratina." They used to drink it during weddings and other party celebrations. Only those elders who had undergone a particular ritual were allowed to drink it. You would hardly ever hear a story of death upon this brew. But nowadays, the central province is leading to the untimely deaths of young men after their consumption of the illicit brews and the second-generation liquors.

In the Rift Valley province, we have many different tribes, and each tribe has its own traditional brews. However, let me focus on one particular tribe, the Kalenjin, because they make up the majority of Rift Valley. They have their favorite brew known as "Maiywek."

DEATH FROM ILLICIT BREW

The Maiywek brew is put in one pot, and the elders would each be seated on a stool around the pot with their traditional pipes in the brew pots. They'd suck the brew with the pipe (straw) from the container.

I love the gospel song, which is a warning to the Kalenjin community by evangelist Paul Kirui of Baringo County. It says in the Kalenjin language, "*mi meet Teret*," meaning, "death in the pot."

The Kalenjins are my friends, and they are blessed with very productive lands in the Rift Valley. But today, they have problems just like other tribes in Kenya. They are becoming alcoholics, and so they are wasting a lot of their time searching for this dangerous illicit brew.

That's why Paul Kirui speaks of the dangers of alcoholism and its effects on society. I love the song because it has a powerful message for the Kalenjin.

I am therefore asking all tribes in Kenya to embrace sobriety and avoid taking this poisonous illicit brew. I'm going to every county in Kenya rebuking deaths from the pots of the illegal brews. If you are a Kalenjin, rather than drinking the illicit brew, you'd be better off drinking the sour milk that you call the "Mursik."

Another dangerous behavior that is associated with alcohol is smoking. Smoking has many health risks. Even the young women and girls are smoking these days. Smoking doubles the risk of heart diseases, lung cancer, and premature deaths.

The sad thing is that millions of people are taking up smoking these days, which is causing respiratory diseases. Smoking is the most significant heart attack risk factor to the victims. It raises blood pressure and contributes to the thickening of artery walls, a condition known as "atherosclerosis." Abusing drugs and smoking both increase the risk of heart disease. They affect the body's blood-clotting mechanism and cholesterol levels.

Apart from the long list of health conditions upon which smoking is a risk factor for both men and women, women smokers risk developing problems of their own. They are prone to a certain kind of lung cancer. Lung cancer is killing many women today. By smoking, women develop cervical cancer because nicotine destroys the cells of the cervix. Smoking destroys the immune system. Women smokers may also develop breast cancer.

Researchers say that women who smoke may reduce their fertility because nicotine may interfere with good egg production. Other risks in women include threats to unborn children. If you smoke while pregnant, you are more likely to suffer a miscarriage, give birth to a low-weight baby, or experience problems during pregnancy and labor. Smoking reduces supply to the fetus, resulting in respiratory infections.

We have started rehabilitation centers in our ministry to minister healing and deliverance to the victims of alcoholism and smoking. Victims are being healed and totally delivered.

Another thing is that alcohol has contributed so much to sexual immoralities and HIV/AIDS infections. The Bible explains that the daughters of Lot made him drunk so that they could have sex with him. They said, "Come. Let us make our father drink wine, and we will lie with him so that we may preserve the seed of our father. And so they made their father drunk that night. The firstborn went in and lay with her father, and he perceived neither when she lay down nor when she rose" (Genesis 19:32).

When a man is drunk, he does not care about the size or the age of the woman he is seducing. Every man is attracted to any woman when he is drunk. Be careful of a drunken man or woman.

Do you want to die from HIV/AIDS? That's why I am encouraging you that if you are married, stick to your spouse. If you are not married, flee from fornication.

The Bible says, "He who digs a pit will fall into it; and a serpent will break through the wall and bite him" (Ecclesiastes 10:8). Do not break the wall of your marriage because the serpent called "HIV/AIDS" will bite you, and you will die soon.

The Bible encourages you, "Drink water from your own well. Should your fountains be dispersed abroad streams of water in the streets, let them be only your own and not for strangers with you. Let your fountains be blessed and rejoice with the wife of your youth. As a loving deer and a graceful doe, let her breasts satisfy you at all times and always be enraptured with her love" (Proverbs 5:5–19). Watch your well, fountain, or other source of water. Evil people could poison your water, and you would die.

That's why I encourage couples to honor their marriage vows, as the Bible says, "Marriage should be honored by all and the bed undefiled, but fornicators and adulterers God will judge" (Hebrews 13:4).

God will judge all adulterers and fornicators. Adultery is a sexual affair between a married person and an unmarried person. Fornication can be defined as simply having a sexual affair with someone who is not married.

You can therefore agree with me that alcohol and drug abuse has contributed to the increase of HIV/AIDS in the world. The Bible says in Proverbs, "Wine is a mocker, and whoever is deceived by it is not wise" (Proverbs 20:1).

When you are drunk, you cannot control your sexual emotions. That's why alcohol and illicit brews are sold by immoral women. Why do these shameless women flock in bars at night? It's because they know that alcohol arouses sexual emotions, and they like to show their thighs openly to men to attract them to sex for hire.

The Bible says that these immoral women are very dangerous. "For the lips of immoral women drips honey, and her mouth is smoother than oil. But in the end, she is bitter as wormwood and sharp as a two-edged sword. Her feet go down to earth; her steps lay hold of Hell" (Proverbs 5:3–5).

Do you want to die from HIV/AIDS? World AIDS Day is commemorated every December 1st, and this year's theme is "HIV prevention." UNAIDS, while releasing this year's theme, stated that despite the progress made against HIV over the past 15 years and the availability of prevention and treatment methods, the annual number of new HIV infections among adults has remained static at an estimated 1:9 a year since 2010.

Moreover, there has been a resurgence of new HIV infections among the youth populations in many parts of the world. An estimated 1.6 million people are living with HIV in Kenya, and new HIV infections are estimated to have declined by about 15 percent in the last five years.

There are an estimated 18,327 infected drug users in Kenya with an HIV prevalence of 18.3 percent within themselves, which is three times higher than the general population.

There is evidence that more and more youths (in primary schools, secondary schools, and higher institutions) are getting addicted to drug abuse.

In this regard, HIV prevention efforts should therefore be targeted at the people who use drugs to implement "harm reduction" programs. Harm reduction refers to policies, programs, and practices that aim primarily to reduce the adverse health, social, and economic consequences of the use of legal and illegal psychoactive drugs.

As we celebrate this year's World AIDS Day, let us strive to invest in harm reduction for HIV prevention and close any HIV gaps among people who inject drugs into their bodies.

God has given me a ministry to reach the youth in schools and colleges before they perish in drugs, alcoholism, and sexual immorality. I am called to give solace, strength, and healing to drug addicts and alcoholics. I'm breaking the bondage of addictions, hopelessness, and poverty in their lives. I have declared that there shall be no more deaths by drug addicts and alcoholics.

I am joining the Kenyan government in their fight against drug abuse. It's hunting for the abusers, and it has banned drug trafficking and illicit brews. The drug campaign patrols and raids are happening everywhere in the country. I'm very serious about the war on drug abuse because I know well of the dangers.

The moment I accepted Jesus Christ as my personal savior I was saved, healed, and transformed. That's why I am telling drug addicts to weep not. "Behold. The Lion of the Tribe of Judah has prevailed" (Revelation 5:5). Jesus is the Lion of Judah. Call on him.

Recently, in Kenya, a mass media reported several deaths in different parts of the country after drinking the illicit brews. The brews used poisonous chemicals, and because the victims could not have afforded to buy the quality brands, they opted to consume the illicit brews. The bad news is that death is in the pot.

The parliamentarians and all people in Kenya cried, "There is death in the pot!" How could I watch these poor victims die without doing something to rescue them before they perish? I thought. A few months ago, I joined the administration in the Lanet division of Nakuru County in a raid-in-Free Area location. The area chief invited me to go with them on the raid. I went in and witnessed liters of the illicit brews being destroyed in the estates of Nyamarutu, Kiratina, Kioundu, and Murogi. We destroyed all cooking pots and everything else connected with the illicit brews. The police ransacked every house and arrested the drunkards and brewers. They were all charged in court.

That's why I say, "Woe to those who wake up early in the morning and search for dangerous substances. Woe to brewers who destroy the lives of the victims by causing deaths and domestic violence in their families." Cursed are the pots of the illicit brews.

My advice to you is to keep away from the immoral women in the estates, who wake up early to make secret trapping nets to catch men with the illicit brews. These wicked women are after your money and manhood.

Remember. If you follow these immoral women, death will follow you like a storm. Your destruction will be coming to you like a whirlwind. Distress and anguish will befall your family.

If you decide not to listen to my message of warning, then prepare for your death, for it will come soon. How do the families feel when they are told to go and collect their loved ones in drinking dens dead?

Today in society, we are witnessing behavioral manifestations of victims suffering devastating problems from illicit brew dependence. In the rural area, I have gained recognition regarding my role in helping society to stop drug abuse.

Drugs and substance abuse is emerging as a serious security challenge. That's why we are transforming drug addicts and alcoholics into sober Christians. The most destructive drug in general use today is alcohol. The recent survey by the National Authority for the Campaign Against Alcohol and Drug Abuse (NACADA) states that children and youth are increasingly using alcoholic beverages.

Alcohol has been destroying many families and plugging men into bankruptcy. It has ruined many lives of children, broken many marriages, wrecked manhood, and caused untimely deaths in our society. The media is advertising that alcohol has power, yet it is precisely the cause of many domestic problems in our homes.

Another cause of the destruction of lives is widespread drug use by our youth. We have many who are using heroin, cocaine, marijuana, and crack. Millions of young people are dying from the abuse of these illegal drugs.

Alcohol is killing more people in Kenya than AIDS. We have an increase in crimes such as rape, defilement, murder, assault, suicide, and domestic violence. You will find the police searching for criminals in the slums, villages, estates, and ghettos.

My father died from cirrhosis, a liver disease caused by alcohol. His stomach and colon became inflamed. The doctor told us that long-term alcohol abuse causes a cancer in the liver, and it destroys brain cells. Alcohol can lead to the formation of peptic ulcers, high blood pressure, a stroke, or a heart attack.

That's why I started a campaign against drug abuse and alcoholism. It is dubbed after the quote, "I shall not die but live and declare the work of God" (Psalm 118:17). I am rescuing the youth and the elderly from death that occurs after abusing the deadly scourge that is sweeping lives across the world. We are rescuing drivers because they are causing more deaths on our highways by driving under the influence.

When I first started to drink, it began as a social act; something that I did to please my peer group. But later, I became hooked into habitual use. I could not sleep without first having either a drink or a puff of a drug locally known as "bhang."

That's why today I am the director of a rehabilitation center that is helping drug addicts and alcoholics to live sober lives. I am using the Bible to elaborate to the abusers about the harmful effects of drinking alcohol and abusing drugs.

"At the last, it bites like a serpent and stings like an adder" (Proverbs 23:32). Alcohol stings like an adder and bites like a serpent. In the market, we have an illegal brew known as "Stings." The media is advertising this brand. However, remember that the Bible says that, "Wine is a mocker, strong drink is raging, and whoever is deceived thereby is not wise" (Proverbs 20:1).

I know well that the best treatment of drug and alcohol abuse is Jesus Christ. Why not resolve today to say, "Lord Jesus Christ, save and deliver me from sins and addictions." Jesus came here to Earth to save sinners and to set free captives (Luke 4:18). He can surely deliver you and set you free from sins and addictions no matter how overwhelmed you may be with them.

You are invited to the Kingdom of God by Jesus Christ as He says to you, "Come unto me, all you that labor and have heavy burden, and I will give you rest" (Matthew 11:28).

In Kenya, people drink illicit brew, which is mixed with a dangerous chemical called "Ethanol." The substance affects the nervous system and interferes with the victim's perception, mood, and consciousness. It makes young husbands unable to perform their responsibilities in their beds.

We are rehabilitating the victims, some of whom are recovering from damaging consequences of drug addiction. Young wives are welcoming this step to rehabilitate their husbands. Drugs and the illicit brews give the victims a false sense of well-being. Afterward, the abuser suffers a lot of pain when he or she tries to withdraw.

In our ministry, we have ministered hope to the hopeless victims. By receiving Jesus Christ as their personal savior, victims are being saved and totally transformed. We have rescued victims from committing suicide and others from depression.

I do seminars for the victims as we give them the full dose of the word of God. We are assisting former drunkards and drug addicts with starting their own income-generating businesses after salvation. We have projects for the youth and the old to alleviate poverty, hopelessness, and joblessness.

We give the former addicts life-changing skills after their deliverance. I give them my personal testimonies, and I encourage them in life. Many former addicts are living drug-free lives now. Many are living as sober Christians. We are giving the former addicts the best treatment for addiction: Jesus Christ.

When I became tired of being an addict, I called Jesus Christ into my life and became totally transformed. Jesus is the answer for all the victims. In my ministry, I lead the victims and the addicts to Jesus Christ, the only savior of the world.

Many victims have been delivered from addictions and diseases. Even those victims with terrible behavioral manifestations and those who are suffering from devastating problems related to drug addiction have been healed and delivered.

My ministry is committed to eradicating the problems of addiction in society. I have full knowledge and experience on how to set free the victims. The church serves the victims without charging them for anything.

We are sharing some spiritual techniques free of charge to any willing person or victim. We are appealing to our government or any willing NGO or person to assist us in making my vision a reality. The church must support the government to fight this illicit brew menace. Through our ministry, thousands of suffering victims are healed, saved, and delivered from addiction.

The success of this wonderful program of rehabilitation is undeniable. In our centers, victims are recovering from signs of withdrawal and symptoms of dependence, e.g., yawning, weakness, nausea and vomiting, or feelings of hot or cold.

I also interview the former addicts. Some tell me they had become totally delivered. Others say they feel helped regardless of what the duration was of their addictions. There is proper healing in the blood of Jesus Christ; it washes away all sins.

After healing, the former addicts are set free from their cravings and their bodies become repelled by the smell of drugs or alcohol. We are reaching the victims in the cities and in rural areas. As Christians, we are welcoming victims into our sanctuary, where they would come running for healing, salvation, and counseling.

The strong faith in Jesus Christians helped many addicts to deter from addiction. I tell the former addicts to abstain. The church is helping all those victims who are in search of deliverance and abstinence.

Throughout the country, our ministry, "Gospel Messengers Church," is leading a campaign dubbed "I shall not die." This is to sensitize the society from the dangers of abusing drugs and the illicit brews.

Good reports have been reported from centers and in our local churches. Our local churches have an interview procedure that confirms those victims who are willing to be delivered. We invite the victims into our rehabilitation centers, and the program kicks off.

The victims are taught the Bible verses before their deliverance, healing, and salvation. Before admission to the center, the victims are required to complete the enrollment forms carefully. The victims should be accompanied by a friend, a spouse, a parent, or a relative to certify the facts on the enrollment form. In the program, the victim would be required to do some physical exercises and learn some spiritual teachings on how to keep their healing, salvation, and deliverance.

The center is sponsored by the church under the leadership of the presiding Bishop.

Anybody willing to support is welcomed. The Bishop is the director of all centers.

We are willing to work with any volunteers or any organizations. Anybody can feel free to assist us in raising funds for the management of the center.

All local churches are required by the director to evaluate the behaviors of the former addict and give him or her moral support. Every center should provide the church with the feedback of every victim and his or her testimony. All former addicts and victims must be welcomed in the local churches. The director expresses his gratitude to the leaders of the center around the country.

On behalf of the church, the director would like to thank all those who are working hard to give hope to the hopeless in this hurting world. The director encourages community participation. We are always busy finding funds and donors who would be willing to support these centers. We are encouraging our pastors in the local churches to demonstrate the pure love of Jesus Christ on the cross by helping victims.

The task of maintaining the centers is indeed taxing to the pastors and the directors. Because of a lack of funds, sometimes we are forced to suspend the services to the victims and resume later. Such unexpected irregularities prevent the church from offering our full potential. We are committed to serving the hurting. Our appeal to society: please help us to give hope to the hopeless in life.

I am ministering life-changing messages to help those with stress-related problems. If you are suffering from those problems, please let us know. For the youth, we have a program in our church to help them in their economic and social development. We introduce them to the digital world by assisting them in networking through the Internet, where they can use computer skills and other essentials skills to make money. Through this program, we eradicate poverty, joblessness, hopelessness, drug abuse, and HIV/AIDS transmission. We have counseling sessions on entrepreneurship ventures and other social problems affecting the youths.

I have written books to help with our outreach program. They are written to encourage victims and give them hope in this world. The titles include *Hope for Survival, I Shall Not Die, Never Lose Hope, Do Not Weep, Love Without Lust* and others.

We have projects in the towns and inner cities for AIDS orphans, as well as feeding programs, vocational training centers for underprivileged youth, rehabilitation centers for drug addicts, and income-generation programs for the hopeless and hurting. My motto in this wonderful group of projects is, "I shall not die but live and declare the works of God" to this hurting world (Psalm 118:17).

While leaders are carrying out their mandates for creating a secure environment for social-economic development, alcohol and drug abuse emerges as a significant social challenge and a threat to national security.

The youth tend to engage in crime as a way of raising funds to sustain their drug-dependency lifestyles. This trend is worrying, and that's why the author is working hard to warn the youth to put this destructive behavior of alcohol consumption and drug abuse to an end. That's why he is transforming drug addicts in his ministry.

Please. Let the word of God through the ministry of the author usher you into a sense of newness in your life. May you have a new beginning and commit yourself to Jesus Christ and repent your sins.

In particular, the youths are the most of whom are affected, which poses a serious threat to the productivity of the working-age group. The youth have formed organized criminal gangs with different names who are operating in villages, towns, and cities. This is a threat to national peace and security.

In this book, the author is calling all the people in our country and in the world to live in peace. He is helping many different types of people to find reconciliation through his peace forums dubbed "Hope for Survival."

"The joy of the Lord is my strength" (Nehemiah 8:10).

CHAPTER FOUR
I CROSSED OVER FROM DEATH TO LIFE

THERE WAS A CONFLICT in the Lanet village when the devil confronted me and prompted me to kill myself before I would achieve my ambitious dream of becoming a preacher. My parents were poverty-stricken and perpetual drunkards. When I became a teenager, peer pressure and evil influence drove me to drug abuse and crime. Sometimes I was locked in police cells for assault. During my miserable life, I attempted suicide. In desperation, I cried out to God as I willingly surrendered my life to Him. I was miraculously delivered from death, sins, and drug abuse. I escaped death by a whisker.

Today, I am a preacher of the gospel who is rescuing youth from drug abuse through seminars and through my greatest campaign against this threatening menace, dubbed **"I Shall Not Die."**

The specific nature of my life was deceiving with so many pleasures and youthful lusts surrounding me. I thought I was enjoying life, but I was actually heading into the deepest hell within my soul. I felt empty and lost.

Many times, the hardships of life accumulated in my soul, resulting in bitterness and resentment. I was exhibiting soul-destroying behaviors and held grudges. Little did I know that drinking changed me and that abusing drugs was taking poison into my body. I was a drug addict.

My life was hopeless. I was overwhelmed by pressures and sins. I was lost with no idea of where I was or where I was going. It was not easy for me to have my life as such a mess. My brother, David, told me to read the Bible. He promised that in it I would find answers for my hopeless life. "What is the world coming to?" I questioned for the first time. Upon reading the Bible, I found that it was full of true stories of people who suffered pain and sorrow, but when they cried to God in faith, they were saved and delivered.

I cried to God by faith and asked Jesus Christ to save me. Jesus came into my heart, and I experienced comfort and real joy. I felt a thrilling power in my soul that changed me completely; from a drug addict into a witness of Christ. My life in this world became very fulfilling, and it will be until the end. Through God's power and mercy, I crossed over from a crooked generation into a chosen generation. My heart was filled with God's praises that gave me the real meaning of life. I was now a pilgrim in this world; not for a period of time, but forever. I started the journey that stretches forward into a more joyous and exciting discovery of what God had in store for me , life eternal.

Are you faced with pleasures and sins that go beyond your control? Whether it is sickness, the loss of a loved one, the loss of a job, or tensions at work or in your relationships? God changed and blessed me with my two brother.You find us going to the church. Peter Muya and David Muya. When we promised to obey God's word, we received blessings our changed lives.No more drugs. We crossed from death to life. I am writing this book as a pastor; purposely to encourage youth to live by faith in God's word so that they, too, may receive such promised blessings.

I'm encouraging the young generation to accept Jesus Christ as their personal Savior so that they can be saved, delivered, healed, and restored. I'm encouraging them to avoid sexual sins or fornication that is causing HIV/AIDS, which is ravaging many families in Africa. Globally, an estimated 36.7 million people are living with HIV, but only around seventy percent of them know they have the virus. It's better to know your status. Our mission involves helping people know what their status is regarding HIV.

In order to face the challenges that remain with HIV, it's important to look for the victims. They are our sisters, brothers, mothers, fathers, relatives, friends, and neighbors. Don't ignore this important information! Get to know the historical facts and statistics so that you can help by showing compassion to those who are infected and help prevent transmission.

Let's look at the global situation and trends present ever since the beginning of this deadly HIV/AIDS epidemic. Let's help people to know their status by receiving an AIDS diagnosis. As a pastor, I will do my part in preventing transmissions for however long HIV continues to be a major global public health crisis. I will educate all communities around me about the facts and give them the entire information on the signs and symptoms of HIV.

Do you know your status? Do you know where you are heading to? Can you be sure that you are heading down the right road in your life? Is your life secure in this world and will it be secured for Heaven? Yes, as a pastor I want to assure you by giving you this important information about your life now and thereafter. All this information is provided in the Word of God.

I want you to be aware of exactly what lies ahead of you. Where are you going to spend eternity? Maybe you don't like this subject or you don't want me to talk about death. And so, you are tempted to turn away at this point. Many people are like that. Even my father did not like to hear about death. He used to be unconcerned about death. Indeed, there is no topic more avoided today in our African communities than that of death; or hell, that place of everlasting fire and torment. However, both death and hell are very real.

My father once met me on the roadside with an old man of his age. I was telling this old man about the need to repent his sins for the final judgment after death. I was discussing this topic of death with the old man, and in response, my drunkard father said, "There is nothing like final judgment! Stop talking about it. I don't want to hear about it." I was really upset when he pulled the old man away and told me, "Let's go! Leave this fool alone!"

My question to you is: "How will you escape death and the final judgment?" Jesus said, "Your serpent, your generation of vipers, how can you escape the damnation of hell?" (Matthew 23:33). You thieve, your generation of robbers, how can you escape the damnation of hell? You adulterers, your generation of war mongers, how can you escape the damnation of hell? Liars, drunkards, prostitutes, hypocrites, and false Christians, how will you escape the damnation of hell? The Bible says, "The fearful, and unbelieving and abominable, and murderers and war mongers, and sorcerers and idolaters and all liars shall have their part in the lake that burns with fire and brimstones, which is the second death" (Revelation 21:8).

Those of you who have scoffed at the Christian faith and ridiculed the followers of Christ have blasphemed the God who made you. If you are married, please don't break your marriage vows or engage in sexual immorality. You young girls, don't have abortions because that is killing an unborn child. You young men, stop abusing drugs and alcohol. Your rich man, stop hoarding more wealth at the expense of your fellow men; stop greed for more gain! How will any of you escape the damnation of hell?!

My father was a perpetual drunkard; therefore, he died a drunkard. Every morning he used to wake up early before drinking his tea to drink a few glasses of chang'aa, the illicit brew. chang'aa was the hiding place from the accusation of his own conscience. It's true that because of alcohol abuse my father was a failure in life.

However, my mother had abandoned the illegal business of brewing and selling chang'aa. She instead embraced religion. She was such a kind woman with a special gift of hospitality. Even though our resources were uncertain, she was very generous. She would always spare a cup of tea and a plate of food for an expected visitor. Visiting relatives would come to stay with us for varying periods of time.

Even though my mother was not drinking alcohol, her most bitter moments were when she'd find out that her loving husband was in the hands of police. My father was often arrested by the police for being drunk and disorderly. My mom paid every penny to free her husband from the jail cells. At home you could hear her defending and rebuking our neighbors who tried to create curiosity and family wrangles by alleging that her husband was a perpetual drunkard.

The truth is that my dad was drinking alcohol every day and his addiction caused kidney failure and "cirrhosis" of the liver, a chronic disease. He would not stop drinking the deadly substance despite the stern warnings doctors gave him.

My father did not believe in God; not even this one day when one member of our church tried to convert him. "Do you want to become a Christian?" the member asked my father. "Yes, at some point," he replied, "but I want to enjoy the pleasures of this world first." My father did not know that he was soon going to die.

My father was admitted to Kenyatta National Hospital for months. Preachers and believers tried hard to convince him of believing in Jesus Christ, but to no avail. A few days after he was discharged from the hospital, he felt the approach of death and passed away peacefully. Little did he know that because of his wrecked life he would be heading to hell, the place of torment. There is no torment known to man so hard to bear and full of anguish and agony as the torment ultimately brought upon by such acts as addiction to drugs and alcohol. My father was killed by alcohol, and now he is spending eternity in hell.

This is why I am asking you to repent your sins right now before you die an untimely death like my father did. Life is ultimately uncertain. Don't lose your opportunity to repent your sins because the Bible says, "Behold. Now is the accepted time. Behold. Now is the day of salvation" (2 Corinthians 6:2). Like many hopeless people in this hurting world, my father thought that he was enjoying life, but instead, life enjoyed him.

This reminds me of a parable about a certain rich fool in the Bible. "The ground of a certain rich man brought forth plentifully. And he thought within himself, saying, 'What shall I do? Because I have no room to bestow my fruits.'" But then he remarked, "This will do. I will pull down my barns and build greater. And there I will bestow all my fruits and goods; and I will say to my soul, 'Soul, you have much goods laid up for many years. Take your ease, eat, drink, and be merry.'"

But God then said unto him, "Fool! This night, your soul will be required of you. Who do will those things be that you have provided?" (Luke 12:16–20 KJV). You fool! Don't reckon with the uncertainty of life and the risk of being dashed into the deepest depths of hell forever. Death is everywhere. In the air, in the sea, and within the earth. Death comes suddenly and unexpectedly. Today you may be fine, but perhaps tomorrow you will be sick. Accidents are on every side nowadays. Danger is everywhere you go. Remember what God told the foolish rich man: "You fool, this night your soul shall I require of you" (Luke 12:20).

I can remember that every year, month after month, week after week, the Spirit was calling, pleading, and beseeching my father to repent but he didn't. The Bible says, "It is appointed unto men once to die but after this the judgment..." (Hebrew 9:27). After your death, what will you tell God on Judgment Day? How will you escape death and judgment?

I was a drug addict and fornicator before I received Jesus Christ as my personal Savior. I believed the Word of God, and I was totally saved, delivered, healed, and restored. Suddenly, I fled from addictions, sins, and sexually transmitted diseases like HIV/AIDS. This great change was made possible only by the blood of Jesus. It was so surprising; not only to my family members and friends, but to all villagers who knew me as a crook. I started preaching to my family members, friends, and neighbors.

My sister, Jane, was born in 1950. She was blessed with her first-born daughter in the year 1968. She went through many unsuccessful marriages until 1976 when she married William. William was working as a building contractor in Nakuru Town. Jane and William were living in Gilani Estate when they were blessed with their second-born daughter in 1981. Since that time, my elder sister and her husband continued to live together despite a history of domestic violence.

One day, I was preaching the gospel to Jane and William in Nakuru Town. William was a perpetual drunkard and a chain smoker. They quarreled and fought nearly every day because they were both drunkards. In 1988, Jane accepted Jesus Christ and joined "Happy Church" in Nakuru Town. In the year 1993 William died. And it was not until later when my sister discovered her husband used to be involved in sexual immorality and, as a result, died a miserable death. After the burial of her husband, my anguished sister remained a Christian.

However, a few years after William's death, Jane was diagnosed with cervical cancer. In her dangerous condition, her temperature was very high. She refused to attend services and weekday fellowship in the town. We decided to take her to our rural home to stay with my mother, who cared for her while she was sick. As a pastor and her brother, we took her to Rift

Valley General Hospital, then Kijabe Hospital, then lastly to Naivasha District Hospital. The doctor there told us that Jane had complications and that she had very few days left to live.

Every day Jane was experiencing physical, emotional, and spiritual anguish, and her unresolved guilt caused her to have uncontrolled anger, self-pity, and feelings of inadequacy. Other spiritual problems included a sense of loneliness, stress, depression, regrets, and a lot of frustrations. In the hospital bed, Jane would cover herself and avoid speaking to some friends and even relatives. She was very rude and violent, and she quarreled with her doctors and nurses. At times, she had a hot temper that would make her very wild and shout outbursts of abusive words to others. She was in the last stages of her life. She died in Naivasha Hospital.

While we may not know what lies immediately ahead of us, we may positively know where we are going to spend eternity. The Bible makes it plain that we can know. "These things I have written to you who believe in the name of the Son of God so that you may know that you have eternal life" (1 John 5:13). "He who hears my word and believes in Him who sent me has everlasting life and shall not come into condemnation but pass from death to life" (John 5:24).

My friend, God, is willing to give you eternal life and turn you into a new creature. Who will deny that today the world is in a more chaotic condition than at any previous time? We have tried our own ways of salvation, but the result is just more chaos. I know many who have made wrecks of their lives. They have tried everything – drugs, fornication, alcohol, sexual immorality—but the end is chaos.

I have the answer to all those who might be asking, "Is there an answer to the many issues of this life?" The answer is Jesus. "I am the way, the truth, and the life" (John 14:6). Friend, why go any longer in your way while Jesus has invited you? Will you continue to endure the chaos and the confusion of this world? Are you aware that you can know your verdict? How can this be? Jesus Christ recorded this truth in the Bible. Read this portion of the scriptures very carefully, as it gives you hope of how you can escape the awful verdict.

"And I saw a great white throne and Him who sat on it. Him whose face the Earth and the Heaven fled away from; and there was found no place for them. And I saw the dead, small and great, stand before God as the books were opened; and another book was opened, the Book of Life. The dead were judged out of those things that were written in the books according to their works. The sea gave up the dead who were in it and death and Hell were delivered up to them as they were judged; every man according to their works. And those delivered with death and Hell was cast into the lake of fire. This was the second death. And whoever was not found written in the Book of Life was cast into the lake of fire" (Revelation 20:11–15).

Notice that the final confirmation of the verdict was not based on the judgment of their works but rather on whether or not their names were written in the Book of Life. I am very happy that after a very tough struggle in the life of my brother, Dominic, lastly his name was written in the Book of Life. Let this be your expectation, my friend, and let your name be written in the Book of Life.

DEATH FROM ILLICIT BREW

My brother, Dominic, was born in the year 1959. He attended Mereroni Primary School and Kiwairia Primary School. He then proceeded to Thika High School. After his O-level examination, he joined Kitui for his A level. During his childhood, Dominic was not initially occupied in his mind by education, but when my grandfather took him to the central province, he embraced it very much.

In high school, Dominic fell in love with the English language, but his favorite subject was science. He was not in a hurry when learning. He struggled until one day he made it to the top. With discerning instincts, you could find that he had a gift in science. He applied what he had learned from doing practices in school and at home. His gentle heart and his wisdom made it possible to pass English and science with flying colors.

Since childhood, Dominic was a committed Catholic. He started teaching English and science in a Catholic secondary school. In 1983, he married his sweetheart, Grace, and brought her home to the Kiambogo village, where our parents lived. The whole family accepted and appreciated Grace; such a beautiful young lady. Grace was married in a customary tradition because my brother did not like the idea of a church wedding. During this time, our father was still alive, and he loved Grace. After she gave birth to a second-born son, according to the African traditions, he was named after Father.

In the year 1991, while teaching in Nakuru Town, Dominic was invited to study biological science in South Africa. For more than ten years, my brother used to come home once a year. His wife and three children were living in Nakuru Town. My brother was a well-respected scholar in his successful career as a senior lecturer in biological sciences at Swaziland University in South Africa. Dominic had many certificates in botanic sciences and many important and authentic documents; that of which every scholar in the world must have.

After having studied and worked in South Africa, Dominic started his projects for his Ph.D. The projects took him to many countries around South Africa to do his research .. Through his lectures and research, he greatly benefited his students. He was a very cool scholar. He was given many awards for his good work in the sciences. Friends and the family congratulated him. He decided to help many students, especially African ladies who were beginning to show interest in the field of sciences.

However, I can give a full, detailed description of Dominic's life not only in education and social activities but also within the consequences of his evil behaviors with alcohol and immorality. During his projects for his Ph.D., Dominic stopped coming home. When I inquired from his friend, who used to visit us, he told me that my brother had become trapped in the grips of drinking and being with women in South Africa. Women are generous in South Africa. And with all this generosity, how could my brother survive? For three years my brother was in South Africa .

Through evil cultural practices Swaziland was leading in immorality and HIV/AIDS in the continent.So you can predict the situation that my brother found himself in that country without his wife..When our sister, Jane, died, my family and I tried to call Dominic home; we also wrote letters through email. But Dominic never responded, so we buried

Jane without him. After three years, my brother finally came home in November 2002, and he became overwhelmed by emotions and cried upon hearing of Jane's death.

When Dominic did come home, he was very sick with pneumonia, which made his breathing difficult. We took him to various hospitals, including Kenyatta National Hospital. Immediately after he was discharged from the hospital, pastors of Deliverance Church Freehold, Nakuru Town, came to see him. After ministering to him and leading him in a sinner's prayer, Dominic accepted Jesus Christ as his personal Savior. Family members, relatives, and friends visited Dominic to encourage him. He decided to join his wife and children at the "Deliverance Church Freehold, Nakuru Town." Gradually, he learned about the word of God, the Holy Spirit, and water baptism.

A few months later, we noticed that Dominic's condition was getting worse every day. The whole family remained very close to him. The shadow of death was now hovering around his bed. My brother lastly cried, "God in Heaven," before he died and went to be with the Lord. His body was rushed to the morgue while the burial preparations started immediately. After a few weeks, we buried him in Nakuru North Cemetery. Thank God that my brother's name was written in the Book of Life. Relatives and friends flocked to Nakuru to comfort Grace and her children. My mother,sisters, brothers, Dominic's children, and all of our extended family members stood very strong during this hard time in our lives.

The word of God encourages us that "Yea, though I walk through the valley of the shadow of death, I will fear no evil, for you are with me. Your rod and your staff will comfort me"

(Psalms 23:4). Upon having to bury her son, my mother was greatly affected by his untimely death. She was reminded of the pain she had felt when she buried her daughter, Jane, just a few years ago.

In the year 2004, my mother accepted Jesus Christ as her personal Savior. She was always praying to know the will of God in her life. She used to always confess her sins loudly before God. She believed that God forgave all her sins even when she could not feel forgiven. Her faith was very strong and unshakable.

After my sister's death in 2000 and that of my brother in the year 2003, I started a campaign against sexual immorality and alcoholism. "No more death from immorality or drug abuse, in Jesus's name." To the couples, I warned, "He who digs a pit will fall into it" and that "a serpent will bite he who breaks through a wall" (Ecclesiastes 10:8). To the married, "Be faithful to your spouse and don't ever break the wall of your marriage because you will fall into the pit of sexual immorality and be bitten by the serpent called HIV/AIDS.

The Bible says, "Marriage should be honored by all and the marriage bed kept pure, for God will judge the adulterer and all the sexually immoral" (Hebrews 13:4). If you are not married, maintain purity and righteousness until the day of marriage. If you are married, stick to your spouse. In this miserable and chaotic life, our God can lead you to practical principles for a "set-apart" life marked by truth, forgiveness, and faithfulness in marriage.

Today, mass media bombards viewers with evil images, which are causing sexual immorality and fornication to be on the rise in the world. God called upon me to warn the world to stop sexual immorality, which leads to HIV/AIDS, and lastly, to death. I am writing this message to all people so that they will know their greatest enemy, sexual immorality, which has killed millions of people through HIV/AIDS. We are tired of burying people. We must know how to combat and overcome unholy urges and cravings how to resist sexual temptations, like Joseph in the Bible (Genesis 3:1–7).

I am conducting a nationwide campaign against fornication, sexual immorality, and HIV/AIDS. My motto is, "I shall not die! But I will live to preach the gospel in this hurting world!" My life-changing seminars have helped thousands to escape death from evil behaviors, evil habits, evil lusts, and addictions. I'm helping families and communities in the villages, towns, counties, and other nations to escape from untimely death. By believing in the word of God, you can find the truth, which will help you to answer hot-button questions about sex and marriage.

In this message, you will find tips on how to avoid sexual immorality. We are burying so many people from HIV/AIDS. That's why I am declaring, "No more death!" The Bible says, "The wage of sin is death" (Romans 6:23). "Whatever a man soweth, that shall he also reap" (Galatians 6:7). The Bible also tells us, "It is appointed for men to die once, but after this, the judgment..." (Hebrews 9:27). If you have not received Jesus Christ as your personal Savior, please accept him today; before it is too late.

CHAPTER FIVE
DO NOT JOIN THE LOSERS IN HELL

I ALWAYS THANK JESUS for calling upon me personally by my name. He is the door that opens both ways. He lets me into safety and protection. He is my shepherd. Through His open door, He lets me in to feed on His table. I drink from His never-failing springs. Living in Jesus does not mean being enslaved or restricted by lists of "don'ts" and "have-toss." Jesus has freed me to live confidentially and adventurously.

Jesus promises me blessings even though I sometimes make mistakes. Whenever I am in danger, I shall not fear, for He will never leave me nor forsake me. He is the door through which I receive divine blessings. He has been encouraging me to enjoy those divine benefits.

Even though I could be passing through the valley and shadow of death, I will not be fearful, for Jesus will see me through. I am not too young nor too old to dream or live with my vision. I will love, thank, and praise God for all the divine blessings bestowed upon me. I'm receiving them.

I'm encouraged by Prophet Joel. One time, a plague of locusts invaded the crops of the Israelites, and intense forest fires shrouded them in despair. The prophet gave them hope in their condition of hopelessness. He called upon the people to kindly ask them to turn to God and trust Him. He said, "Return to the Lord, your God, for he is gracious and merciful" (Joel 2:13).

In the people's state of wilderness, Joel prophesied blessings and abundance. God poured out His Holy Spirit upon all the people; young and old. Therefore, they started to dream, hope, and love, as well as thank God, for God was faithful to them. In my wilderness, Almighty God will lift me up, and I will dream, hope, and love, as well as thank my God for His faithfulness.

God gives the living things in the deep seas and deep oceans food to eat in due season. If He were to hide His face from these creatures, they would surely become dismayed and die.

I am always trusting God, for he has given me assurance that I will live forever in His presence. I'm happy to say, "My redeemer lives," and I will never forget the precious death of my father! He joined the losers in hell! "Fare thee well. father" My family gave our father a beautiful send-off!

From the beginning, the word "hell," seems to have become filled with a very highly respected class of sinners, like the rich man written in the Bible (Luke 11:19). Hell is a place of consequences for a sinful life. I am writing this message with sorrow because my father died a perpetual drunkard, and there is no doubt that he had been dashed into hell with the rich man.

I know you would shrink in horror if you were to be told upon death that you would be condemned to hell. Do you know that Jesus loves you, and that He does not want a single soul to perish in hell? Make plans now to register yourself in the Book of Life in heaven by repenting your sins and accepting Jesus Christ as your personal savior.

"And whoever was not found written in the Book of Life was cast into the lake of fire" (Revelation 20:15). The question is: Is your name in the Book of Life? Remember that on the day of judgment, God will find you whether you were dead in the sea or on the earth. The sea will give up the dead who are in it, and death and hell will be delivered upon the dead who were in it, as they were judged, like every man, according to their work. This is the second death (Revelation 20:13–14).

There are different deaths. There is the natural death that will happen to everyone on earth. However, there is also the second death, which is where unrepentant sinners will be thrown into the lake of fire and tormented forever.

I am always happy to know that I shall not die the second death. My mission in this hurting world today is to declare the works of God in this crooked generation. I was shocked when my father died suddenly because I knew that he would be cast into hell. When I remember how my father died a sinner despite many warnings from Christians, I regret. My father ignored the gospel and everybody who preached to him when he was alive, but now in death he cannot ignore God's judgment anymore.

I am preaching the gospel because I don't want people to be dashed into hell. I am doing everything I can to make sure that I save as many sinners as I can before they perish. My father died an unrepented sinner, and nothing can be done to save him now. His sins will have led him to where he was destined to be. When I remember that place of torment, I increase my warnings to the sinners.

Question: Are you going to allow yourself to become condemned to spending eternity in hell like my father and that rich man? This story stirs my heart to preach as never before.

My message is simple. "Repent therefore and be converted, so that your sins may be blotted out and that times of refreshing may come from the presence of the Lord" (Acts 3:19). I am preaching these messages of eternal life and eternal death to sinners and to believers. I am witnessing the great things God is doing in my life and ministry.

I preach the gospel before large gatherings of young people. My message to you is to come to Jesus Christ now so that you will be totally transformed from one of this crooked generation into one of a chosen generation. I thank God that I am now of a chosen generation.

God's love will keep the record of every person and his or her deeds. One day everybody will give an account of their life and deeds. Remember that the way that leads to destruction is broad. Are you aware of the reality that sooner or later you will die? Are you getting prepared for what will happen after death? Receive Jesus Christ today to escape hell. Blessed will be all those who die in Christ. They will go to heaven, and their works will follow them. Turn to Jesus, who can save you now. There is still time yet for you to begin a new life—but after this????

I tremble when I think of the coming day of judgment – I know how soon it will come. What a fearful time it is when I think of the day when the son of man will appear from the clouds from Heaven as foretold in the book of Revelation. "And I saw a great white throne and He who sat on it; from whom the earth and heavens fled away. And I saw the dead, the small and great, stand before God, and a book was opened; and then another book was opened, which was the Book of Life. The dead were judged out of those things that were written in the books according to their works" (Revelation 20:11–12).

As I write this, I know many will soon find themselves in hell with the rich man. Who is the rich man? The Bible says there was a certain rich man who was clothed in purple and fine linen and fared sumptuously every day. There was a certain beggar named Lazarus who was laid at his gate full of sores and desiring to be fed with even the crumbs that were left from the rich man's table. And it came to pass that after the beggar died, he was carried by angels into Abraham's bosom.

When the rich man died, he was buried but then entered torment in hell. He lifted up his eyes and spotted from afar Abraham and Lazarus in the bosom. The rich man cried and said, "Father Abraham, have some pity! Send Lazarus over here to dip the tip of his finger in water and cool my tongue. I am in anguish in these flames." But Abraham said to him, "Son, remember that during your lifetime you had everything you wanted and Lazarus had nothing. So now, he is here being comforted, and you are in anguish. And besides, there is a great chasm separating us. No one can cross over to you from here, and no one can cross over to us from there" (Luke 16:24–26).

Let me tell you openly that every person needs a hiding place for his or her sins and a hiding place from the accusations of his or her own conscience. A hiding place from the cunning of the devil; a hiding place from the wrath to come. The question is: Have you found a hiding place? If not, flee from your sins today and come to Jesus Christ.

Jesus is standing at the door of your heart, knocking. Allow Him to enter into your heart. Listen to His voice that is speaking to you saying, "Come to me all you that labor and are heavily laden, and I will give you rest" (Matthew 11:28). Will you come now, or will you wait until Jesus comes? Repent now, and Jesus will free you from sins; and you will be saved.

In memory of Dad, I imagine him crying in the deepest depths of hell; wailing, weeping, and gnashing his teeth, saying like the rich man, "I am tormented in this flame" (Luke 16:24).

Through His mercy and love, God intervened in the life of our poverty-stricken family in the late seventies. David, my elder brother, was the first to be saved. One year later, after observing my brother's changed life, I also accepted Jesus Christ as my personal savior. At home, I usually sat beside the fire in the morning and in the evening reading the Bible to my younger sisters and talking about heaven at every given opportunity.

My father used to drink the illicit brew called "chang'aa," even though it wrecked his health. Ultimately, he died of acute kidney failure and a disease called "cirrhosis." He died a miserable sinner. I looked at his dead body and wondered, *is this the same father who had jokes and laughter last night when we had a cup of tea together?* "Poor Dad. I wish you knew that your death would be so sudden and that God is real. You would have confessed your sins. But now, it's too late for you." That is what I said as I paid my last respects to my father as the relatives slowly hovered his body into the grave.

Never was there a moment so awful to me as looking down at my father in a coffin. He lived as a drunkard, and he eventually died as a drunkard. If you read the Bible, you would know the fate my father had coming to him. After my father's burial in 1984, I started writing this book to warn the drunkards, the drug addicts, and other sinners not to allow themselves to be dashed deep into Hell like my father and the rich man.

Suddenly The Fire Fell From Heaven.

Despite the great work of man in scientific advancement, the world is still in bondage of sins, suffering in shame. The need for salvation is great because man will always be a slave of Satan for as long as the virus of sin is rooted in his senses and conscience. The devil led my father into the slaughterhouse (hell), making him dance in the fire crying, like the rich man.

Sin is a heavy burden in your life, and you would not dare to take the risk if you understood its danger. The wage of sin is death, as in the second death, which means to be dashed into hell forever; total separation from God. Do you want to trust God now, or wait until trouble, tribulations, or adversity strikes? It might become too late if you wait to trust God.

Remember this. Fire suddenly fell over the plans of Sodom and Gomorrah. Fire fell upon the people without warning. They laughed, but they did not know about the lake of fire that laid deep beneath their feet. A massive accumulation of gas and sulfur deposits exploded and engulfed them, with the fury from the outraged wrath of God, and they all died without warning.

Can you remember the first atomic bomb in human history suddenly exploded over the Japanese town of Hiroshima, resulting in mass deaths and extensive damage that terrified mankind? The message to Asia is more straightforward: repent or perish.

Kenyans will never forget the July 8, 1998 bomb blast in Nairobi city, which left many dead and many others helpless with serious injuries. The message is simple to Africa; God loves you. Repent of your sins and receive Jesus Christ as your Savior.

America was suddenly attacked by terrorists on September 11, 2001. They hijacked an airline and crashed the planes into the World Trade Center, causing an explosion and fire; killing almost 3,000 people and injuring over 6,000 more.

The whole world lamented about this awful act of terrorism that caused fear to fill up within many people in America and in the world as a whole. The message is simple to Americans. Don't be like that rich man. Repent, America.

Father Joined The Losers in Hell.

I remember how my father used to wake up very early in the morning to search for the illicit brew called chang'aa in the village. Don't be like him; he is now spending life in hell. Trust in Jesus in your life always, and you will escape my father's fate.

My father and the rich man are losers in hell. Don't join the losers. Live in Christ, and you will live in heaven forever.

A word of advice to children in our family

It's only a few of you who knew your grandfather and I am sure that you hardly remember his enticing voice in cracking jokes with you. He used to laugh with you; but you will never meet him again. He is in hell, and if you don't repent now, you'll probably join him there. Don't emulate your grandfather because when Christians and preachers persuaded him to repent, he promised them that he would repent "tomorrow," but that "tomorrow" never comes!

Indeed, you never met with him, your great grandfather. Let me tell you a brief history of him. Your grandfather lived a reckless life drinking liquor far too much. He died suddenly without having repented his sins. And he now resides in the deepest depths of hell with the rich man. Please repent now while you still can.

A word of warning to the villagers who knew my father.

I know you will always remember escorting your departed kin. He ate with you and laughed with you. But now, he is long gone. When he was here in this world, he did not repent his sins. Now he is in the realm of eternal torment, that horrible place that was made for the devil and sinners.

Keep on enjoying life in your festivals and parties, but if you don't repent, you will be with him one of these days. Hell was not made for you; there is hope for you now if you receive Jesus Christ as your personal savior. This will make you live a useful and holy life in this world.

Will you be dashed into the deepest pit of hell because of your unbelief? Repent now or otherwise perish. Don't be like the rich man and my father. My friend, death is inevitable to all of God's creations. So, when it eventually knocks on your door, where will you spend eternity?

The story of the rich man stirs in my heart, and it constrains me to be more diligent in persuading men to repent. Don't be like my father, who fooled himself by thinking that he would seek salvation after death when he instead became surrounded by eternal fire everywhere in hell. He is crying in anguish with the rich man right now.

I'd say, "Goodbye, Father. Rest in peace. You will be remembered by your children, grandchildren, neighbors, and relatives."

These are the memories of my father. After his death, I started an outreach project to warn the drunkards, drug addicts, and other sinners not to condemn themselves to hell like my father and the rich man. Repent your sins. Join me in this outreach project, and your life will never be the same again. Don't join the losers in HELL

A Word Of Warning To Our Students.

God has given me a ministry to rescue the students in colleges, universities, and schools, as well as other youths, from drug abuse. teens are a target of the drug peddlers, and drug abuse is causing the destruction of properties in schools and colleges of higher learning.

I advise the youth to maintain a good relationship with others and with their teachers. It is essential to learn how to properly and appropriately handle disagreements with their teachers to avoid strikes and destructive acts. Are you a student? Such bad behavior will greatly affect your performance and your well-being as a student. A good work relationship with your teacher is healthy, and you should work towards these objectives.

As a student, you must understand who you are in Christ. If you accept Jesus Christ as your savior, you can overcome stress and frustrations. Respect your teachers and learn to communicate your problems with your seniors effectively.

Trust in yourself and in Jesus Christ. Be humble; do not be aggressive. Be a positive thinker. Have a good time to relax. Learn to listen and understand the needs of others. Trusting in Jesus Christ will help you to overcome stress, which is very common with students. The word of God energizes, motivates, and helps believer students to overcome challenges in their lives in school and at home.

Stress can cause severe psychological and physical problems. High levels of stress can lead you to depression. Are you tempted to try drugs or alcohol to overcome your stress? Be realistic in dealing with your present problems.

Are you anxious, irritable, or stressed? Are you losing interest in life or in your studies? Are you feeling tired all the time? Do you feel like withdrawing socially? Do you have trouble concentrating? You could be suffering from stress!

Call Jesus Christ now in your soul and confess all of your sins before Him by faith. You will receive peace and joy in your heart. Jesus is the answer in your troubled life.

Through seminars, we are reaching the youth in the villages, estates, slums, and ghettos. We are transforming drunkards and addicts into sober Christians. We are eradicating poverty by creating jobs for the youths by encouraging them to start income-generating projects and small businesses.

I am teaching former addicts and abusers how to face reality as I save them from depression, stress, frustrations, hopelessness, poverty, joblessness, and committing suicide. I am giving the youth life-saving skills. Many youths are being delivered from drug abuse. They are being restored and transformed. I am changing hopeless youths into victorious Christians and business people.

This book is written with the purpose of helping the hopeless and the hurting youth with concise and informative features that address their problems. After reading this book, I am sure that your life will never be the same again. Thousands of youths have been set free from death, sins, and addictions. Join me in declaring, "I shall not die, but I will live to declare the works of God in this hurting world!"

I know now that you have the answer. After your death, where will you spend your life in eternity? I was a drug addict. My life was a mess and miserable. But when I decided to accept Jesus Christ as my personal savior, I was totally delivered and transformed—from a drug addict into a gospel messenger.

Jesus made my life come alive after granting me eternal life. He became the author of my destiny. I learned to sing praises and worship songs in the church instead of the sad secular songs I used to sing with tears in my eyes.

Let me tell you openly that whatever choice you make now will determine your destiny. The wrong decisions may be eating you up already. Yesterday's choices are today's memories and suffering. If you are going through any painful experiences right now, it is because of the choices you had made before. Are you suffering in bed from HIV/AIDS because of your choice in committing sexual immorality?

No matter what the circumstances are in your life right now, there is still hope for you. Just choose Jesus Christ as your personal savior now, and He will instantly turn your life around. He will save, heal, and deliver you from all manners of sins, bondages, diseases, or addictions. It is not too late.

One choice you make today can mend the whole of your life and your generation together with you. Make the decision right now to accept Jesus Christ as your personal savior, and you will enjoy the fruits of the Kingdom of God. You will never forget the day you made this ultimate decision.

When I accepted Jesus Christ as my personal savior, He taught me the joy of winning souls. Today I am a soul winner, and I move in rhythm with His beautiful plans and His wonderful steps. He is leading me day by day in my ministry through the Holy Spirit and the Word. Choose life!

Naturally, life is full of ups and downs, but I came to realize that they're results of the choices we have made. God has helped me to mature up in the Christian faith to the point of choosing something in life; and not just something, but a good thing like eternal life and other spiritual blessings.

God has given me the freedom to choose what I want. "I call Heaven and Earth to record this day against you, which I have set before your life and death, blessing and cursing. Therefore, choose life, so that both you and your seeds may live" (Deuteronomy 30:19).

The decisions I make today will not affect me alone, but as God puts it, it will affect me as well as my seed—as in my generation. The decision you will make today, my friend, will affect not only you but also your generation. Every day in your life, you will encounter many issues that will cause you to make choices that will determine your destiny in life.

That's why I boldly state that I am a product of my own choices. Many people today blame their parents for where they are in life. However, let me tell you openly that whatever happens in your life should not forecast your future.

Remember. God encourages you to choose life and live, but many today are repeatedly choosing death knowingly. Therefore, you are a product of your bad choices. Let me say that all those people who will go to heaven are those who have chosen to be wise, while those who will go to hell have chosen to do so. In this context, no one is really "forced" to go to hell or heaven. You make the decision to choose either life or death.

Today, when you hear the voice of God through these words—Please! I beg you not to harden your heart. As the Holy Spirit says, "Today, if you will hear His voice, do not harden your hearts" (Hebrews 3:7–8). Make a choice and accept Jesus into your heart. Make heaven your future home, and your life will change completely.

You have freedom of choice. Will you go about doing whatever you want? God has given you power and freedom, but this freedom should not be abused. Instead, it should be taken positively, and making the right choices will bring you eternal life through Jesus Christ.

Just because of your freedom of choice, should you choose sexual immorality if that's what you desire, where you'll likely end up dying of HIV/AIDS? May God forbid! You should make good choices. Don't choose death and curses by living in sexual immorality. Choose life and blessings in Jesus Christ, our Lord and Savior.

Since the day I accepted Jesus Christ as my personal savior, I declared like the psalmist that "I will not die but live and declare the words of the Lord" (Psalm 118:17). When I accepted Jesus Christ, I was delivered from sins.

I openly declared, like Joshua, that in my life, I have chosen to serve God with all my heart and strength (Joshua 24:15). I publicly declared the choice I had made as far as God is concerned. Today there are millions of people who have not openly declared what they believe or what they stand for. You cannot tell whether they've really been born again or not. They appear to fit in with both believers and unbelievers. They are neither hot nor cold. They are lukewarm. "So then, because you are lukewarm and neither cold nor hot, I will vomit you out of my mouth" (Revelation 3:16).

In this hurting world, God is looking for those believers who will openly declare of whom they are serving. You cannot afford to pretend anymore. You will pay costly for pretending. You better declare your stand openly. Let your belief stand out.

You can choose to act or react when you are in a fix. You can either respond positively or negatively. As for me, I will always respond positively, no matter what it is I'll go through. How would you choose to respond if you if you lost a loved one from HIV/AIDS? How would you feel on the day of the burial when you'd see your father, mother, sister, brother, auntie, uncle, or other relative in the casket just before the moment he or she is lowered into the grave? How would you act or react?

Some people think they are the only ones going through whatever pain they are going through. Whatever you are going through happens commonly to other people. So, you see, it all depends on you how you choose to respond.

God has given us two incredible things: the absolutely awesome ability and freedom of choice. The tragedy is that many people in this hurting world have abused this ability and freedom. Are you one of them? God has given you the right to choose. Choose life and blessings, and you will live forever. One person said that successful people are failures who have chosen never to fail again.

In the midst of darkness, God can make you discover within you the invisible light that is still there. Go ahead by faith, and you will see what God has set before your life and blessings. He wants to give your life. Choose life so that you may live. Your whole generation will be affected by your choice.

I don't preach the gospel in this hurting world because I have the answers. I preach because God has given me the message. I was born to win souls for Christ. And if I don't win souls for Christ, I might miss the reason for my existence. It's my highest desire and joy to win souls for Christ in this hurting world.

That is why I am telling the whole world, "Choose life today." You have the freedom and will. Don't care about what the devil may have put before you. God has good plans for your life. You may not know what the future holds for you, but you'll know one thing. You can choose to make your life either better or worse.

Let me find you there in the church praising and worshipping the true God. Think before you make any choice in your life. Even if you were born under curses, that does not mean that you'd have to live your whole life under those curses. Jesus carried away your curses on the cross. You are the blessed of the Lord.

Even though I was born in an alcoholic family, that did not automatically mean that I would ultimately end up dying an alcoholic, like my father did. Jesus set me free from alcoholism. I became a born-again Christian.

Even if you were born under a specific curse—you name them. Theft, drug addictions, witchcraft, cancer, etc. The choice to inherit any of these lies within you. You can choose to either continue the curse or break it completely.

If any curses have been following your families, this is no guarantee that you will also inherit them. Choose life today. God is calling witnesses to see what you shall choose. God is calling upon the attention of his whole creation, and heaven and earth, to see to the decision you will make.

I desire to always serve God and be ready to meet Jesus Christ when He appears. I am standing like Joshua openly declaring, "As for me and my house, we will serve the LORD" (Joshua 24:15).

I will never forget the day God helped me to choose life through Jesus Christ, who died for me on the cross. "Love is strong as death" (Song of Solomon 8:6).

Today, my mission is to give hope to the hopeless in this hurting world. I declare, "I shall not die but live and declare the works of God" (Psalm 118:17). That's why I am changing this crooked generation into a chosen generation. The Bible warns, "For if you live according to the flesh, you will die, but if by the Spirit you put to death the deeds of the body, you will live" (Romans 8:13).

The decision to live or to die is yours alone. Choose life, and you will live. If you die without Jesus Christ, where do you expect to spend eternity? Please, do not join the losers in Hell..

CHAPTER SIX
MY CAMPAIGN AGAINST ILLICIT BREW CONSUMPTION.

MY GRANDMOTHER TOLD me that traditionally in the Kikuyu community alcohol consumption was restricted to elders of a specific age-group. Alcohol was utilized during a forum to exchange news, resolve disputes, formalize marriages, etc. Alcohol was for a group and not for an individual. The elders used to drink together in a party for happiness and socializing.

The Kikuyu used fermented alcohol known as "muratina," and for the Kalenjin, "busaa." These fermented alcohols were less destructive to the body because they had a lower alcoholic content, as opposed to the modern brew, which is mixed with Ethanol. As little as ten milliliters (ml) of Ethanol can cause blindness or optic nerve damage. Thirty ml is potentially life-threatening. One hundred ml is fatal.

The consumption of alcohol is written in the Bible. It is a custom that has been tolerated among many African communities. Some of the second-generation brews containing methanol are legally accepted but are causing harm to the abusers and society.

Misuse and abuse of alcohol and drugs has resulted in deaths, blindness, and widespread domestic violence, divorce, and road accidents. The abusers are experiencing the progression of symptoms. Alcohol consumption is a social behavior that is destroying both the youth and the old. Unemployment and alcoholism are challenges for our teenagers.

Recent studies in the Lanet Division by our project team showed that alcoholism and drug abuse have resulted in various health-related problems, including sexually transmitted diseases. Prostitution, abortion, and suicide are widespread in the area. A woman was collected dead in a bar, while a young man committed suicide. A newborn baby was saved from a pit latrine after it was thrown in after birth. Many people have died as a direct consequence of alcohol consumption. Despite regular raids by the administration in the Lanet Division, statistics show that alcohol consumption is increasing.

Are you affected by the impact of alcoholism? Are your family members and neighbors complaining? Who else is suffering as a result of your drinking? How can you prevent your children from imitating this destructive behavior? Alcoholism destroys victims financially, mentally, emotionally, and spiritually.

In the slums and ghettos, alcohol and drug abuse are contributing to crime. In these areas, the initiation age for alcohol and drug abuse is about ten years. I am helping the youth before they hit rock-bottom. I am willing to go out and reach out to all affected youths and plant a seed of hope that can have positive results for their lives now and for all eternity. I want to preach the gospel now as never before to the youth. Jesus is greater than your present problems.

The Alcoholic Drinks Control Act 2010 states that all alcoholic drinks are to be packaged in glass bottles of not less than 250 ml and to carry health warnings as well as unit labeling. This is to ensure that drinks are packaged in a hygienic manner and with accurate content information displayed on them.

It is also a measure to reduce the number and frequency of incidences of alcohol-related deaths due to the adulteration of alcoholic drinks. Some previous incidents have been due to the inclusion of methanol in alcoholic drinks packaged in plastic containers. These substances have killed many people.

The government is prohibiting the sale of alcoholic drinks in sachets or in containers less than 250 ml to limit the underage members of the population from accessing such beverages. Health warnings and messages labels must also be included on drinks.

Many deaths have been reported in the country due to the consumption of illicit brews. In one case, thirty people died in Nyandarua County and more than fifty in Kiambu County.

The Alcoholic Drinks Control Act 2010 provides for the control of the manufacturing, sale, consumption, distribution, and promotion of alcoholic drinks in Kenya. It provides licenses and regulations. The Act contains measures to deal with product safety, control of access, and exposure to alcoholic beverages by people under the age of eighteen years. The authority has also managed to sensitize chang'aa and busaa brewers. The traditional brews have to be legalized by NACADA.

I appreciate the Lanet Division administrators for inviting me to take part in their raids. A few years ago, I was glad to join them in what they termed as Rapid Response Initiative (RRI). They sometimes call the district administrators for reinforcements to sustain the operations of the raids.

When I witnessed the raids, many drinking dens were destroyed and brewers arrested. Thousands of liters of the brew were destroyed. The abusers fled in terror, and only a few were arrested. The challenges are many in the area, but the administrators are fighting to end the vice.

At the national level, alcohol abusers deplete the human resource base, thereby reducing economic productivity. Alcohol abuse causes poverty. It increases the national burden of diseases like HIV/AIDS and reduces life expectancy. Evil behaviors related to alcoholism and drug abuse are central to HIV/AIDS infections. Thousands of alcohol and drug abusers have died out of HIV/AIDS.

I'm comforting and encouraging the widows who have lost their husbands to alcoholism. I remind them of a widow in the Bible who was accompanied by relatives and neighbors as she was crying and weeping for the death of her son. Her husband had died, leaving her very lonely with only her son. The son died, and suddenly, the grieving mother met with Jesus.

Jesus comforted and encouraged the crying mother, "Don't cry." Jesus called out to the dead boy, "Get up." Life returned to the lifeless boy. Jesus presented the newly resurrected son to the rejoicing mother. The mother, relatives, and her neighbors praised God for performing this miracle.

When you were a child, did you ever see your mother cry? I have only two memories of my mother crying when I was young. She told my brothers and I that as boys, we should never cry. Mother used to rebuke us, telling us, "Men don't cry." She wanted us to be in charge and to be strong men.

Today I am encouraged by the words in the Bible, which show that Jesus wept over the city. He wept before he was taken to the cross until you could see drops of blood streaming down from his face. The tears that Jesus shed were not of satisfaction from achievements or tears of joy for winning the Olympic gold. His tears were of intense suffering because of people's sins.

Today I am weeping for the drunkards dying from the illicit brew. Thousands are dying before they repent their sins. Therefore, they are going directly to hell.

Jesus wept for his best friend, Lazarus. He was dead, but Jesus called him back to life, and it was done. Jesus carries our sins and burdens, and that's why he is inviting us, "Come to Me, all you who labor and are heavy-laden and give yourself to Me."

I am a role model for the youths in this hurting world. My two daughters learned to be mothers by watching their own mother. My son learned to be a father by imitating me. All my children learned about life through us, their parents, as well as from other adults.

God requires that as a husband I am to remain faithful to my wife. And as a father, I must take care of my family. And as a pastor, I must preach the Word to my family. When I fulfill such requirements, I keep my commitment to God.

My father was not a role model; he used to sell some of our few items at home at a throw price for a bottle of chang'aa. He was desperate to quench his thirst. Unfortunately, he died a hopeless death.

The Samaritan woman in the Bible wanted to quench her thirst in prostitution. Her thirst was deep in her soul. When she went to fetch water in the well, she met Jesus at the well. Jesus offered her living water, and she was refreshed in her soul and life.

Jesus is willing to quench your thirst now. Unless your thirst is quenched by Jesus, it will never go away. Don't allow yourself to remain thirsty.

The Samaritan woman had tried to quench her thirst with prostitution, but it would not go away. My father had tried to quench his thirst with the illicit brews, but it did not go away. He died thirsty.

Jesus makes an offer to you. He says, "Whoever drinks the water I give will never thirst. Indeed, the water I give will become a spring of water welling up eternal life" (John 4:14). All those who are thirsty in this hurting world, call Jesus Christ into your soul, and your thirst will be gone forever.

Before I was saved many years ago, I led an evil gang of drug addicts in the Town of Nakuru. I was a very difficult young person. Gradually I was becoming overwhelmed by drugs and the illicit brew called chang'aa.

When I became sick of living in such hopeless ways of life, I accepted Jesus Christ as my personal savior in 1978, a step that completely changed my life for the better. From first being a drug addict, I was transformed and delivered into a gospel messenger in my village and out from a crooked generation into a chosen generation.

A few years later, I was appointed as a full-time pastor, and I was given a church branch within Gilgil Full Gospel Church. Deep in my heart, I felt the suffering of drug addicts. Therefore, I started an outreach program to reach drug addicts and other sinners with the gospel.

The outreach program was dubbed, "I shall not die." I began ministering to the physical, emotional, and spiritual suffering of the victims of drug abuse. Many drug addicts are abandoned by their wives and family and are living a hopeless life in loneliness, stress, frustration, condemnation, joblessness, and depression.

Alcoholism

The consumption of illicit brews and other alcoholic drinks is as old as mankind. It is a custom that has always been tolerated by African communities. Although legally accepted, alcohol has the potential to cause harm to the consumers if abused.

Traditionally, alcohol consumption was restricted to the elders of communities. It provided a forum to exchange news, conclude communities' agreements, resolve disputes, and formalize marriages. The older drank for fun and happiness. Most African communities consumed fermented alcoholic content as opposed to the illicit brews and other alcoholic drinks of today.

Sadly, the drinking of alcoholic drinks has lost its traditional values because it has been commercialized. Drinking by teenagers has gained prominence. Alcohol consumption is a social behavior embedded in communities' cultures and has many determinants.

Alcohol abuse refers to the misuse of alcohol that results in problems for the abusers and those they may affect. Consequently, abuse does not necessarily indicate alcoholism. Alcoholism involves developing a dependency on alcohol and follows a somewhat predictable progression of symptoms.

According to numerous studies, biological factors have a significant effect on the progression from experimentation to regular use, and social and cultural factors play a critical role in experimentation with alcohol and the development of drinking patterns over time.

Given this evil behavior's social nature, it is not surprising that alcoholism causes many problems in families and communities. It has health-related issues ranging from sexually transmitted diseases to obsession with smoking, bed-wetting, and even suicide. Many traffic accidents are related to the abuse of alcohol. Alcohol abuse is a significant contributor to the country's morbidity and mortality statistics through poisoning, road accidents, and homicides.

At the national level, alcohol abuse depletes the human resource base, thereby reducing economic productivity and exacerbating national poverty due to poor use of money and wasted hours.

Alcoholism increases the national burden of disease and reduces life expectancy. Behavior associated with alcohol abuse is central to HIV infections and complications of AIDS management. According to a report tabled in Parliament in August 2010, a total of 143 people were reported to have died as a direct consequence of alcohol consumption. Yet despite these shocking statistics, alcohol consumption has increased by nearly 50% over the past generation. And each of the millions of alcoholics negatively affects four to seven other people.

There is no way to put a shilling figure on the emotional agony suffered by alcoholics and their families and co-workers. I am not writing for Kenya alone because I know that alcoholism is a prevalent problem in other nations of Africa as well.

As I write, I know millions are being impacted by alcoholism. I understand that some of our brothers and sisters have problems with drinking alcohol but deny it. Denial is one of the primary symptoms of the affections, and the issues of alcoholism thrive in an atmosphere where knowledge and awareness are lacking.

Many misconceptions, misunderstandings, and prejudices about alcohol abuse are rampant in our societies. We should know how to deal with perpetual abusers and heal their prolonged suffering. There are many painful experiences of alcoholism. The Bible warns, "There is death in the pot."

The introduction of the second-generation brews and other illicit brews like chang'aa has even worsened alcoholism in Kenya. And as a consequence, the country has witnessed widespread consumption of alcoholic drinks, especially among youths. The survey conducted by the "National Campaign Against Drug Abuse Authority" in 2007 indicated that 13% of the Kenyan majority who were between the ages of fifteen and forty years consumed alcohol, and the most abused alcoholic drinks have been the "second-generation brews," which are mostly packaged in plastic bottles or sachets and sold to anybody, including young boys.

All these illicit brews are causing premature deaths, blindness, bed wetting, impotence, and other health complications to their consumers. The misuse or abuse of alcohol in the country has resulted in severe socio-economic consequences, e.g., widespread domestic violence, insecurity, rape, defilement, corruption, HIV transmission, increased road accidents, reduced economic production, and a drop in good academic performance in schools and colleges. I teach the youth how drugs contribute to HIV infections and how they can be set free from drugs.

Drug Abuse

Drug and substance abuse is emerging as a serious security challenge. As a result, Kenya has been serving as a transit point for narcotic drugs from countries involved in drug trafficking. These drugs include cocaine, opiates, heroin, mandrax, and cannabis. I was an addict to cannabis because it is locally cultivated around Lake Naivasha, Kisii, the central highlands, and along Uganda and Tanzania.

Alcoholic Drinks Control Act 2010

The government enacted the "Alcoholic Drinks Control Act 2010" in an attempt to bring sanity to the alcohol sector. The law's objectives are to protect the health of consumers from excessive consumption of alcohol, prevent those below the age of eighteen years from accessing alcoholic drinks, and promote treatment and rehabilitation programs for addicts. The law provides comprehensive control of the manufacture, sale, consumption, distribution, and promotion of alcoholic drinks in Kenya.

My Outreach Program

The problem of alcoholism and drug abuse is beyond the legal approach alone because it affects everybody. It is a social problem. As a pastor and former addict, I am very much concerned. I am conducting an outreach campaign against alcohol consumption and drug use dubbed, "I shall not die."

The old adage, "An ounce of prevention is worth a pound of cure," is certainly true concerning alcoholism. You must recognize the symptoms and signs of developing alcoholism. You should not let anybody drive under the influence.

We are helping our children in schools and colleges through public education and sensitization programs on the effects of alcohol and drug abuse from the villages up to the national level.

Alcoholism involves a downward progression to the barrel's bottom – medically, financially, emotionally, and spiritually. It is 100% fatal if not addressed. Many victims never pull out of this syndrome.

Those victims coming to us for help are doing so only after hitting the bottom. Some are brought to us by caring families and others by friends. With the help of God, we are ministering to the victims until they are saved, healed, delivered, and restored. And we are helping former addicts to start income-generating projects after showing signs of full recovery.

Rehabilitation Process

As a pastor, I wish to reiterate that the fight against drug abuse and the consumption of illicit brews is a joint venture that must be handled through team work and partnership with the government, the church, and well-wishers.

The treatment and rehabilitation of addicts should be instituted as a matter of national priority. Together with all stakeholders, we are going to bring sanity to the alcoholic sector as we give healing and transformation to the addicts.

Join me in the fight against drug abuse and alcoholism. Our rehabilitation center in the church is different from others you may know. We are using the Bible to help victims to re-examine themselves. We are targeting young men and women from ten to thirty-five years of age. This is because many young people experiment with drugs and ignore the fact that it could lead them into an addiction, which is very hard to treat.

Our first concern in this center is recovery from drug addiction. We encourage the victims by promising them a new way of life through Jesus Christ. It is not until the victim comes to our center that the recovery process is possible. The victims enroll to start this recovery process. With much love, they must accept that they are addicted and need help.

The victims are taught step by step the dangers of drug abuse and addictions. The desire to be set free is the basis of recovery from addiction and substance abuse. With the help of the Bible and prayers, victims are delivered and set free from drug abuse and alcoholism. They are taught how to maintain their healing by praying and fellowship with other believers in the church daily.

Step to Full Recovery

1. You must admit that God has power over alcohol and drugs
2. You must understand that God has the power to heal and restore you to sobriety
3. You must commit your life totally to God before and after deliverance
4. You must join follow-up groups in the church
5. You must humbly and always accept Jesus Christ as your personal savior
6. You must go to every person you might have offended or harmed before you were healed and saved
7. You must confess to others how you were healed and

saved to encourage other victims to come for healing
8. Carry the good news to the family, neighbors, friends, and other addicts

In our rehabilitation center, we are also being helped by former addicts who are giving addicts their living testimonies before they pray with them for healing. And this center is expanding to other villages and counties.

We are using Christian videos, musicians, and evangelists to attract all ages to our outreach meetings. Our willingness to transform the lives of addicts has improved the quality of many lives and many families in the communities.

After every successful outreach meeting, the rehabilitation sessions, counseling sessions, and HIV/AIDS sessions begin. We have practical topics and lessons on how to recover because recovery is a process. Are you terminally addicted? Addiction is a disease. Are you a drug addict? A sex pervert? A person living with AIDS? Are you a slave of Satan in any way?

If you are a sinner in any way, the future can look dark and very hopeless. "Eternity" is a terrifying word to think of when one feels he or she is standing on its brink. Do you know that God, in His infinite love, has permitted you to come to His extremity, that He may make Himself known to you? Please, believe this. Typically, it is only when human beings get into hopeless situations that they finally become open to listening to God's voice from His servants.

As a former hopeless drug addict and now pastor, I can assure you that out of your present distress, our caring God can bring you the most remarkable deliverance you could have ever known in your life; just believe!

The Bible encourages you that, "And whatever things you ask in prayer, believing, you will receive" (Matthew 21:22). Jesus is inviting you to ask for salvation and your healing now! Will you?

If you could just believe, God's hand is stretched out to touch you at this very moment with salvation and healing power. All you need to do is to receive Jesus Christ by faith in your heart. He will never release any of His healing or salvation power if you do not ask for it. Will you ask for it?

I know you are part of this worried and anxious generation, which is almost at the brink of death because of sins. I will never blame you, but I know one day you will blame yourself. Despite man's great work in scientific and technological advancement, men and women in this world are still in bondage to sins, suffering, and shame.

The need for the salvation of souls from sins, evils, and addictions is great. Man will continue to be a slave to sin for as long as the virus of sin is flowing deep in their veins, senses, and conscience.

Can you see that you are a hopeless sinner and that your conduct is terrible in this hurting world? If you are trapped in sins and addictions, you are bound by the devil, hand and foot. You are a doomed person who shall be expecting to be dashed deep into hell forever.

In the Bible, there is a brief description of hell. There'd be endless weeping and gnashing of teeth because the fire will be burning sinner's day and night. Sinners will be crying like the rich man, saying, "I am tormented in this flame" (Luke 16:19–24).

To escape going to hell, you must receive Jesus Christ as your personal savior. I am asking you to declare with me, "I shall not die, but I will live to declare the works of the Lord" (Psalm 118:17). We should not be like the people of Sodom who ignored God's word and indulged in all kinds of evils and sins. The fire fell from the heavens and consumed them. They cried, but it was too late for them.

A glance of faith at the Calvary marks on Jesus Christ's body will silence your every excuse. Receive Him now in your heart, and you will experience the power of salvation and healing. Please don't join the losers in Hell.

CHAPTER SEVEN
I AM MORE THAN A CONQUEROR

IT WAS THE MONTH OF April 2021 after the curfew and lock down. My life was thrown into uncertainty after I experienced a severe fever and cough. My family and neighbors suspected that I had all the symptoms of COVID-19. "Could these be the symptoms of the virus?" people wondered.

For two weeks I remained in bed using painkillers, but the pain persisted. That's when my sister, Beth, and her husband developed a plan to help me overcome the pain in my body. Promising to Pay the bill for me, they asked me to consult my doctor, who gave me the prescribed drugs.

When I used the prescribed drugs for three days, my health improved, and the pain was no more. God used my sister to help me overcome the pain. I was passing through the fire of affliction, but, through God's grace I received my healing.

The Christians in my church prayed for me as I stood strong during those two weeks of severe fever, despite a lot of scoffing and mocking from neighbors. I thanked God for all those who helped and encouraged me.

My family was wondering in uncertainty, for they had never seen me sick before. "Could you be suffering from the virus?" neighbors mocked. As a pastor in the village, I have learnt how to endure different kinds of reproach and mocking from villagers. My positive response to my circumstance made me feel better rather than bitter.

I was hoping for victory in the midst of my storm. God has His own ways of doing things. He met me at the point of my need.

Whether I had COVID-19 or not, God healed me. I thanked Him, for I knew that I had survived death. Like the apostle, Paul, I do believe that when I am weak, I am strong. I overcame my problem because of trusting in God. God told Paul, "My grace is sufficient for you, for My strength is made perfect in weakness." Read 2 Corinthians 12:7–10.

In my life I learnt practically to take pleasure in infirmities, in reproaches, and in distress, for Christ's sake. I have learnt to embrace my thorn in my flesh, accepting insults, hardships, temptations, and difficulties in my Christian life.

I have learnt to rejoice in the storm and in pain. The word of God encourages me that when I am weak, I am strong. Although the media was alerting us that the third wave of COVID-19 was spreading very fast in the five counties in Kenya, I believed God for healing. It was not clear whether or not the virus had stricken me, but when I believed in God, my health took a different and unexpected turn. Praise God, I was healed.

I thanked God for my family, for they kept their guard and care up while the church members prayed for me. Even though my situation had inspired mixed feelings in my family, church members, and villagers, God healed me. In my life, although I had been suffering in pain, I could not allow my case to trigger assumption, falsehood, rumors, or myths. I disregarded my feelings and focused on God for healing. However, although I believed in God, I did not stop taking the prescribed drugs. There are temptations in your Christian life, and you must trust in God to help you know how to overcome such things.

The Steadfast Love of GOD Never ceases

For two weeks I was struggling in and out of bed with severe fever, but when I prayed a simple prayer, God healed me. When I remember what God has done for my life, I thank Him. The word of God came to me: "It is of the Lord's mercies that we are not consumed, because his compassion fails not" (Lam. 3:21–22). Then a few lines of the song, "The Steadfast Love of the Lord," flashed in my mind. "The steadfast love of the Lord never ceases, His mercies never come to the end, and they are new every morning, new every morning! Great is thy faithfulness oh Lord, great thy faithfulness!"

This song was ringing in my heart; it encouraged me and gave me hope for a bright future. I received my blessings as the sickness fell down at my feet. I came to realize that those words of the song had encouraged me, given me peace in the midst of my difficult circumstances, and promised me strength. Because of it, I found new hope in my overwhelming situation. I was discouraged, confused, and weary, but God ministered to me in His own way. I turned my eyes away from the storms around me and gazed upward instead. God heard my prayers. I started living by faith and thanked God for His mercies. "They are new every morning" (Lam. 3: 23).

God was walking beside me each day, and He gave me strength to face that trial. Even when the future looked dark and uncertain, He encouraged me, and I pressed on. God assured me that, no matter what was happening in my life, He had good plans for me. I praised God that day for knowing Him, who is greater than the storms of life. He is great enough to me that I trust Him.

Since that day I learnt to encourage myself in the Lord like David in 1 Samuel 30:6. As I thought about the encouragement that I needed during the storm, my mind went to David. He encouraged himself in the Lord even when the people spoke of stoning him. David's example put me to shame.

At that time, I felt discouraged in spite of having the Bible in my hands, a Christian church that I attended weekly, a loving wife and loving children, and many Christians, friends, pastors. and Bishops. With all these blessings in my life, how could I be discouraged? The devil caused me to focus on what I did not have, instead of focusing on all these blessings that I did have. The solution was found when I surrendered my own self to be crucified with Christ and to die with Him. When I did this, I experienced the new power and spiritual victories in my life.

I turned my spiritual eyes away from the problems and every destruction and instead focused only on Him, who is my all in all. Having my own self crucified enabled me to hear the voice of God like Elijah (1Kings 19:12). The still voice was saying, "I am the Lord who heals you!" This voice was very strong, for it overcame the noisy world. God personally called me to step away from the crowd and listen to His voice. I found peace and rest in my troubled heart. By hearing His voice, I was encouraged, and I learnt to encourage myself in the Lord.

I am encouraging others to keep on hearing the voice of the Lord, the Rhema word, in this noisy world of today. You can overcome every situation like David and I did. Praise His wonderful name!

The whole world was lamenting with a pang of sorrow due to the millions of deaths and infections caused by the global pandemic known as COVID-19 or Coronavirus. Coronavirus is the cause of severe acute respiratory syndrome.

The virus was first identified in December 2019 in Wuhan, China. The World Health Organization declared a public health emergency of international concern regarding COVID-19 on the 30th of January 2020. Millions and millions of cases have been confirmed, and millions of deaths globally.

The COVID-19 virus is transmitted when people breathe in the air contaminated by droplets and small airborne particles from an infected person. The risk of transmission through air droplets is highest when people are in close proximity, but it's safe to breathe over longer distances, particularly indoors. Transmission can also occur if splashed or sprayed with contaminated fluids in the eyes, nose, or mouth, and rarely via contaminated surfaces. People remain contagious for up to twenty days and can spread the virus even if they do not develop any symptoms.

The pandemic has resulted in significant global social and economic disruption, including the largest global recession since the Great Depression.

The World Health Organization (WHO) is working closely with global experts, governments, and partners to rapidly expand scientific knowledge on this new virus and to provide advice to countries and individuals on measures to protect health and prevent the spread of the outbreak. Although the WHO continues to tackle the multiple impacts of the COVID-19 pandemic, the virus has pushed millions of people to extreme poverty. The virus is worsening the already difficult situation of older people in society every day.

People globally are talking about COVID-19. However, I am asking people to get their facts and information from reliable sources, e.g. community health workers and doctors. Equitable access to safe and effective vaccines is critical to ending the COVID-19 pandemic. So, it is highly encouraging to see so many vaccines proving to be effective and going into development.

The WHO is working tirelessly with partners to develop, manufacture, and deploy safe and effective vaccines.

Safe and effective vaccines are being discovered by experts, but in order for us to survive and get a chance to see the foreseeable future, we must continue wearing masks, cleaning our hands, ensuring good ventilation indoors, physically distancing, and avoiding the crowd. We should all be vaccinated and not throw caution to the wind by putting ourselves or others at risk, particularly because research is still ongoing to find the most effective vaccines, which could completely kill the virus, boost immunity, and prevent community transmission and deaths.

Let's hope that the WHO will soon give us the good news that they have got the vaccine that will fight the virus once and for all. As Christians, we are praying for the WHO to get the vaccine that will be the hope of the world that gets people vaccinated in large numbers in order to finally overcome this fatal virus. The government must ensure fair and equitable access to vaccines in order to protect its people, starting with the most vulnerable.

In Kenya, we've experienced shocks and pain that are caused by the COVID-19 infections, which had increased dramatically in the past years. It appears that the circumstances that had played out last years are being replicated. If we are not careful will can go back to lock down, where we experienced severe economic stagnation, social disintegration, depression, cessation of movement, curfews, and high levels of poverty and hopelessness.

"Whereas the foregoing measure will have adverse effects on the economy and constrain our unusual way of life, the measures were temporary and necessary to contain the spread of COVID-19. I am convinced that the cost of not acting now would be far greater. One life lost is one too many." That is what President Uhuru Kenyatta had said in Kenya.

The president tightened the COVID-19 restrictions. Kenyans were forced to embrace new ways of living in order to survive through the COVID-19 pandemic period. Other people were left wondering.

Bars ceased operations while hotels served only take-away orders. Public gatherings such as weddings, funerals, worship, and sporting activities were outlawed. Physical learning in schools and colleges stood prohibited, and institutions were required to transit to online teaching.

The pandemic had caused so much tumult because infections and deaths had risen to unpredictable levels. Health facilities were stacked to the limits paradoxically; this came at a time when the world was rolling out vaccination.

DEATH FROM ILLICIT BREW

The questions that are being addressed: For how long will this pandemic destroy lives? Will these vaccines really prevent deaths from the virus? Which vaccine will be our hope in this hurting world?

We are living in real fear of the COVID-19 virus because it is ravaging lives globally, and we have been experiencing deaths here and there in our country. Indeed, the whole world is reeling from development, which is ironic, considering that the virus mutated whenever vaccines that were supposed to restore our hope were produced.

The government had heightened security and health surveillance along the borders amid years when the mutated variant of COVID-19 from India was to circulate in our country. The discovery of the mutant variant had put the country's COVID-19 mitigation measures at crossroads, given that scientists suspect that the variant might be capable of reducing the immunity received from natural injections and vaccinations.

A variant was a form or version of a virus that differs from the original one. The new variants were highly transmissible and were suspected to be resistant to some of the immune fighters. With time, I think many variants will be discovered, putting the country on high alert.

Many people in the world are not aware that we are standing between death and life. We are in the last days. We are fighting a very dangerous virus that can render impotent vaccines. Nevertheless, let's keep observing and following safety protocols to contain the virus and keep it from spreading. Let's trust in God because in Him everything is possible.

The new wave of the virus should be a wake-up call to the researchers to conduct in-depth studies to give us new methods of combating COVID-19. We shall keep on social distancing, washing our hands with soap and water, using hand sanitizers, and wearing face masks until further notice.

We have nothing to do to free ourselves from the new variants, which seem to be more deadly than the original COVID-19 variant. It is clear that we are in the depths of the more waves of the COVID-19 virus. Not a day goes by without the devastating news of the loss of a loved one or somebody well known to us.

We see deaths from the virus in our communities. We are living in great fear. We were staying one meter away from each other. We were wearing masks and sanitizing regularly. It's a new world alien compared to how we conducted things some years ago and it came to be known as the "new normal."

Many people lost their jobs, and thousands of businesses closed down. Business people were left complaining about the difficult conditions they were operating in. Some were saying that if the situation persists, more businesses will be closing down.

The World Bank report on the social-economic impacts of COVID-19 on households was terrible. The rise of unemployment and the decrease in the labor force was severe and long-term consequences on households' welfare. Many companies warned workers on the basis of hardships caused by the virus. May God give people survival tactics.

Fear over the spread of the dreaded Indian strain of Coronavirus, which was vaccine-resistant, was growing. It made many nations, including the United Kingdom, put

Kenya on the red list. Traveling from Kenya to the UK had been restricted. In the statement announcing the decision, the Nairobi-based chief of protocol from the UK ministry of foreign affairs said that some people in Kenya are testing positive for the deadly Indian or South African strain of the virus.

What should we do now? Our news bulletins and our social media feeds were filled with messages of "RIP" with pictures attached to messages of people who we knew very well.

In our homes, to be honest, COVID-19 had broken many marriages. It had negatively affected our sexual lives. How should we treat sex in our marriages during this Coronavirus era? Couples wondered. Life in our marriages changed; it was quite hectic that time.

Before COVID-19, our relationships with our wives was very sweet and hot. But in those days, because of the Coronavirus, life became very cold and dull. Life was full of suspicion, and many spouses were left wondering whether they were to wear face masks when enjoying sex in their bedrooms.

Suppose my spouse is not faithful in our marriage. Should I not allow myself to be at such risk of getting the virus? Yes, I desire sex, to be touched and loved, but my dilemma is, what if my partner is positive? Should I choose not to get infected as well? Which protocol should I apply in the bedroom so that we can enjoy sex without fearing my spouse is infected?

Because of COVID-19, many marriages were going downhill. Many wives at home were demanding basic commodities their husbands were unable to buy because they were fired in their places of work and therefore they could not afford to buy food for their families, like.

As a pastoral counselor, I advised couples to trust God and strive towards achieving life goals. This is the best way to have a successful relationship. No matter what comes in your marriage, let love and faith in God rule your marriage, not materialistic things.

Due to COVID-19, many women were suffering from relationship insecurity, which made them demand things that would safeguard their feelings, without necessarily considering the absolute financial status of their husbands.

It's always better for a husband or wife to sit down and iron out issues instead of jumping to silly solutions like denying his or her spouse rights to sex. This is breaking many marriages. The question is whether or not your marriage was in a downhill because of COVID-19, Sit down with your husband or wife and consult.

Do not drive your marriage to where you know you will hit a bump. Drive your marriage carefully and smoothly with a lot of care to your partner. Couples should stop struggling in their marriages. There have been a lot of suspicions and mistrusts in relationships. The kind of love spouses used to demonstrate in their beds is now fading. The number of deaths from HIVAND AIDS in our friends, family members, former classmates, and colleagues is causing us to develop a phobia for having sex at home. May God help our marriages during these hard times.

Every day we are receiving terrible news on our phones; every time deaths occur from COVID-19 or HIV AND AIDS. The truth is, in a group of ten, three could be carrying the virus. Therefore, it is important that we keep our guard up, avoid situations that aggravate the speed of the spread of the virus, and, most importantly, take care of those we love. We should also encourage the vulnerable, especially those above fifty-eight years of age in our society, to consider taking the COVID-19 vaccine.

I know this virus has brought a lot of mixed feelings and reactions in our marriage relations in our homes, but we must not base our decisions on suspicion, rumors, or falsehood. Let's guard our spouses and children. We should set a good example by providing a vaccination drive in our area.

Our organization, "Christ's Ordained Kids" a Community Based Organization which was working closely with the government to encourage churches and parents to be vaccinated. We also helped to stop the myth surrounding this vaccine in our area. We took one more step to save ourselves from the virus and save those we love.

During the lock down, my organization worked with parents in Nakuru city to pull out children from the gravity of high rates of teenage pregnancy. Many girls aged between fifteen to nineteen were reported to be pregnant or have had a child already. We are alert to discourage premarital sex among our teenagers. And parents should not resist talking to their children about sex, reproduction health, or sex education. They should create good relationships with their children so that they can open up to them about it.

Let's give the girl child the hard truth about her sexual life. Share open conversations to guide a girl child away from a potential unplanned pregnancy. The number of girls sitting for national exams is increasing every year. The lock down exposed our girls to sexual activities. In school, I encourage the teachers to embrace their role of being faithful peer educators to our children. Everybody everywhere should be involved with saving our children from premarital sex instead of condemning them to it. Let's empower them with comprehensive sex education that will help them make informed decisions about their sexuality and relationships in a way that would protect their health.

During the lock down, you could see children begging for money on the streets, others working on the farms for hire, others hawking, and some girls having sex for money. Many young girls were exploited sexually, leaving them pregnant while others got dangerous diseases.

As for the boy children, you could see many abusing drugs or consuming alcohol. Others were trafficking drugs from estate to estate to make ends meet. Let's teach the boy child his rights by giving him the basic needs, like shelter, food, clothing, and health care. Let's create a time for our boys at home to warn them about drug abuse, premarital sex, and other evil behaviors.

COVID-19 has caused a lot of problems in our families. Men have turned to the consumption of alcohol in order to try removing their stress when the wives ask about how they can solve their domestic issues. The husband hurls insult and even tries to beat his wife up. Domestic violence at home could be caused by several issues, including emotional stress and depression.

What matters most in our marriages is love. But perhaps now your husband or wife is hurting, either mentally or physically, because of COVID-19 phobia. I would kindly ask couples to pray to God for wisdom on how to handle certain issues until they are solved. The couples need time to heal after resolving these issues. If in any case there is no solution found for your marriage issue, you can still disclose the issue to both sides of your family and try to mend your marriage before it breaks.

Another emerging issue that is caused by COVID-19 is the face mask disposal menace. A lot was emphasized on how to put on face masks, but we should be informing society on how to dispose them after use.

Everywhere you went you could find used face masks thrown away carelessly. In mutates and streets you could not fail to see one or more used face masks dropped and others being blown away by the wind. This infectious waste could lead to more harm in other people's lives. There was need to be taught better disposal methods to cope with huge numbers of face masks which was being thrown away inappropriately. Since face masks cannot be recycled, we should be guided on the best ways to dispose of them after use to avoid poor disposal, which turns used masks into a menace.

My delight is to write an irresistible story that will inspire you and help you to answer your question of, who will survive in these evil days of incurable pandemics and diseases. The Bible tells us, "Men's hearts failing them for fear and the expectation of those things which are coming on earth for the powers of the heavens to be shaken" (Luke 21:26). Verse 27 says, "Then they will see the son of man coming in a cloud with power and great glory."

The signs that we are seeing is proof to us that Jesus is coming. Jesus has every solution for every one of our problems. For those of us who do not want to repent your sins and believe Jesus Christ as your personal savior, the day of the Lord will come suddenly, it will be horrifying, and devastating. It is difficult for me to describe the horror that will be experienced by the unbelievers on the day of the Lord. People tend to think about God when something horrifying happens in the world, but they soon forget as time goes by. This day, people will be eating, drinking, marrying, and doing all kinds of businesses.

As for the believers, Jesus has given them enough warnings for them to be prepared. For them, it will not come as a thief, but rather it will be in the twinkling of an eye. The Bible says, "Where beloved seeing that you look to such things, be diligent that you may be found of Him in peace, without spot, and blameless" (2 Pet. 3:14).

Because Jesus Christ is coming soon, ask the question, "Where do you want to spend eternity?" Could you be among those who are asking because the conditions are very tough right now? Then, "Who will survive?"

The answer? All those who believe in Jesus Christ now will survive. Through Jesus, survival is possible, now and thereafter. I will never forget the day God saved me, and He called me to serve Him as a pastor. Through Gods love I was transformed from a hustler to an evangelist, later I became a pastor and lastly I became a Bishop.

That's why I'm encouraging you, Never Lose Hope, with God nothing is impossible. Please believe in Him, and you will be saved from your sins and from eternal death. Call Jesus Christ to save you now. "Neither is there salvation in any other. For there is none other name under heaven given among men whereby we must be saved" (Acts 4:12).

CHAPTER EIGHT
I AM IN THE RACE

I WAS BORN AND BROUGHT up in this crooked generation. I was born in the kingdom of darkness. I was a slave of sin in the kingdom of Satan. But now, I am a new person. My sins separated me from God. When the time came ins which I realized I was a sinner walking into the deepest pit of Hell, I called upon Jesus Christ to save me from my sins. Jesus came into my heart and cleansed me by his precious blood. I became a completely new creation. The Bible encouraged me, "Therefore, if anyone is in Christ Jesus, he is a new creation; the old has gone, the new has come" *(2 Cor 5:17)*.

After my salvation, the pastor in charge of my local church organized a water baptism service for all of those who were saved the following Sunday. The pastor said that Jesus had commanded his disciples to be baptized by immersion. He quoted, "Therefore, go and make disciples of all nations, baptizing them in the name of the Father and of the Son and of the Holy Spirit" *(Matthew 28:18-19)*.

We were taught what water baptism is all about. We were made to understand the key to a victorious and liberated Christian life. I understood the term, "to be 'baptized.'" It means to be "totally immersed" in water. After proper teaching, we were taken to the river some kilometers away from the local church during a Sunday service in which we were baptized one by one in water.

To me, this personal thing of going under the water and rising back up out of it demonstrated the real practice of dying to sin. When I rose up from under the water, I declared that I was now a new creation in Christ. The power of the resurrected Christ was now working in my new life as it never was before.

I received the power of the Holy Spirit to allow others to witness it. I told my friends that the pastor had performed my burial service. I was buried, as my sinful nature was buried under the water through the baptism, and then resurrected together in Christ as a newness of life.

The Bible says, "All those who were baptized into Christ Jesus were baptized into his death. We were therefore buried with him through baptism into his death" *(Romans 6:3-4)*. "After I was baptized, my mind was set up for things above and not on earthly things" *(Col 3:1-2)*.

After my water baptism, I declared to all my friends and relatives that I was now a chosen generation. I realized that my old life with sins was put to death and that now I had a completely new life to live in Christ. Nowadays, I teach the believers about the importance of water baptism. The Holy Spirit inspires me to teach the importance of repentance in the life of a believer. After repentance, the Holy Spirit comes to dwell in the life of a believer. The Bible says that "This promise of infilling the Holy Spirit is for us, our children, and all who are far off; for all of whom the Lord, our God, will call" *(Acts 2:38-39)*.

When I was filled in the Holy Spirit, I was able to overcome "the lust of the flesh, the lust of the eyes, and the pride of life which comes from the world" *(1 John 2:16)*. Thank God, for He is faithful to deliver me from all the temptations of the Devil. One of the most eye-opening, soul-searching verses that I have read that encourages me in my life and ministry and sends chills up and down my spine is, "You are a chosen generation, a royal priesthood, a holy nation, His own special people; that you may proclaim the praises of Him, who called you out of darkness into His marvelous light" *(2 Peter 2:9)*.

My greatest call in life is to win souls for Christ. That is why I go out to where the sinners are. I am a chosen messenger of Christ, as "You have not chosen me, but I have chosen you and ordained you so that you may go and bring forth fruits and that your fruit shall remain" *(1 John 5:16)*. I am chosen and ordained to bring forth fruits. Jesus had saved me to fulfill a special task in the world. I am called to win souls for Christ, because "as my father has sent me, I also send you" *(John 20:21)*.

Jesus has called us to go out to win souls. He has warned us not to be weighed down with cares of this crooked generation. He said, "Be on guard so that your heart may not be weighed down with gluttony and drunkenness and worries of life; and that that day comes to you suddenly like a thief for a trap" *(Luke 21:34)*. I was living without hope in this crooked generation, but I suddenly crossed over from a crooked generation into a chosen generation. The real joy and the real peace in my heart today makes this day of my new birth unforgettable. However, with this being my first experience of new birth, I had to learn to adapt to the new setting of life as a Christian; I did quickly.

Today I preach about this new birth and the wonderful experience of salvation to my friends, relatives, and all those who are ready to hear about Jesus. I am on the race to Heaven, and I am a stranger to this crooked generation. I am not of this world, as I am moving towards my destination. I am a citizen of Heaven. God has given me wonderful promises. Jesus said that "He went to prepare for my mansion in Heaven" *(John 14:14)*.

There are wonderful verses in the Bible that are meant to provide great comfort to all believers in this world. Jesus has assured me that He went to prepare our mansions in Heaven and that we are invited guests in the Kingdom. That is why in my Christian life I keep on exercising my faith muscles as I run, with perseverance, the race that is marked for me. I am pressing on by God's glory.

The Bible encourages me, "Let us run with perseverance the race that is marked out for us, fixing our eyes on Jesus the pioneer and founder of our faith" *(Hebrews 12:1-2)*. I am in the race, and that is why I am fixing my eyes on Jesus Christ. Jesus has promised to help me in winning that race, as I am hoping to win it. In the scripture, we are told that, in this world, it is not all fast runners who win the race. The author of these verses was a preacher who showed the reality of this crooked world. The preacher in Ecclesiastes shows us that having success in everything will not depend on our own effort, but rather upon the power of God. God chooses the winner in every race. You will realize that, in this world, "it is not the fast runners who always win the race" *(Ecclesiastes 9:11)*.

Kenya is known by the whole world for producing the best athletes in various international races. We have very many gifted and talented young men and women who win gold, silver, and bronze medals. Any of those athletes may have come from one particular community in Rift Valley Province. From Kenya, as well as from many other communities, God had chosen race winners. In order for them to win the races, they are trained to keep time and to obey the rules of every race. All of the athletes are expected to start well, but the determining factor is the finish line. The Bible teaches us that "an athlete who runs in the race cannot win the prize unless we obey the rules" *(Tim 2:5)*.

The scripture shows us that all believers are in a spiritual race. We are chosen to run the race and win. That is why we are expected to follow the rules. We are in the race, and a large crowd of witnesses surround us. So, "let us put aside everything that gets in the way, as well as the sins that hold us so tightly, and let us run with determination the race that lies before us" *(Hebrews 12:2)*.

I am keeping my eyes fixed on Jesus Christ, from whom my faith starts and ends" *(Hebrew 12:2)*. I will pull every weight so that I may run very fast and win the race, and I will trust in Jesus because He is faithful to keep His promises in my life. I will never be sidetracked nor distracted by anything. I will keep pressing on and finish the race and win. The race is not easy. That's why I have to put my trust in Jesus Christ to strengthen me in the race. My redeemer is encouraging me to continue on in the race until I manage to win my crown, and that does not fade.

Question: Are you in the race? Call Jesus to enlist you in the race. Are you discouraged in the race? Ever losing hope? Call Jesus, and He will help you be a true and faithful athlete who follows the rules of the race. Jesus Christ is our coach. We are surrounded by large crowds of witnesses. Remember.

All believers are in the race, and large crowds of cheering fans surround us on every side of the track. Let us obey the rules of the race.

Let us therefore run with perseverance the race that is before us, fixing our eyes on Jesus Christ. Run, focusing on your destination, to the finish line, JESUS in Heaven!

CHAPTER NINE
A CHOSEN GENERATION

AS I GREW UP SPIRITUALLY, I became a very successful soul-winner in the village church. I was a young evangelist with a consuming desire to proclaim the good news to the sinners. I had given my life to God as a living sacrifice, and He is using me for His divine purposes.

In the year 1979, my pastor, Rev. Mbugua, selected me from the small congregation in the village church to attend a soul-winner's seminar, which was conducted by the famous international evangelist, Dr. T.L. Osborn, and his wife in Nakuru Town. As this man of God taught from the Scriptures, I sensed the clarity of the gospel as he exposed the real state of my spiritual life. I saw my own pride and arrogance. God used the revelation of the Word to break me down and humble me for His glory. The gospel become very real to me as the evangelist taught the value of soul-winning, which was the main topic of the seminar. I was built up and encouraged.

At the end of the seminar, the evangelist prayed for us. As he laid his hands on me, I was slain in the Holy Spirit for hours. When I gained consciousness, I found myself on the floor of the big tent praising and worshiping God in the Spirit. When I returned home to the village church, I realized I had received a double portion of the anointing of winning souls for Christ.

As I testified about what the Lord had done in my life during that seminar in the village church, the Holy Spirit came down onto the small congregation and believers were revived and encouraged. I started open-air meetings in the village with the help of a team of young people in the church, and Rev. Mbugua assisted me with a portable prayer and amplifier, both of which were given to him by T.L. Osborn. Every day we were winning souls for Christ and the church grew. Men, women, and children were saved as they were invited into the church.

My life became very different, for I was always out winning souls for Christ. The Lord was confirming the messages of the cross with miracles. I preached, with signs following. God is faithful. I helped many villagers to overcome poverty and also to find new life in Jesus Christ. The Bible encouraged me to observe the three important things in life: faith, hope, and love. As the Scripture says, "And now abide faith, hope, and love, these three; but the greatest of these is love" *(1 Cor. 13:13)*. My vision was to reach the unreached.

Faith

I was living by faith because I was now a chosen generation. "But you are a chosen generation, a royal priesthood, a holy nation, in that you may proclaim the praises of Him, who called you out of the darkness into his marvelous light" *(1 Peter 2:9)*. I was chosen a generation out of the crooked generation.

I read in the book of Hebrews, Chapter Eleven, about the strong faith of the men and women of God who survived in this hurting world; it encouraged me. I was encouraged by the great man of faith, Abraham, who pleased God by his faith. God credited Abraham as being righteous because of his faith. I knew that I was also credited as righteous on the same faith. "And if you are Christ's, then you are Abraham's seed and heir, according to the promise" *(Gal. 3:29)*.

I have written books on faith: *A Chosen Generation, Obeying My Vision, Blessings of Obedience, the Gospel Messenger, and Repent, Africa.* I am living by faith to achieve my most cherished vision in life of reaching the unreached and giving hope to the hopeless in this hurting world. I know God will make my vision come to pass even though it tarries. I will trust in the Lord forever, for He is my everlasting strength. I will cast all cares upon Him, for He cares for me.

As one whom his mother comforts, so will the Lord comfort me. He will keep me in perfect peace because my mind is focused on Him. Through His divine power, He will give me all the things that pertain to life and godliness. By faith I will speak and confess what I believe; this is what Caleb did, and he possessed the land. I believe in this believing and possessing business.

I am more than a conqueror (Romans 8:37) by faith; I have learned to overcome my troubles, fears, and worries in life through the blood of Jesus Christ. From time to time, I like to pray, study the Word, and make fellowship with other believers. I like to relax in the presence of God. By the power of the Holy Spirit, I am strong in the Lord.

I am looking forward to celebrating the soon second coming of our Lord Jesus. What is faith? "Now faith is the substance of things hoped for and the evidence of the things not seen" *(Heb. 11:11).* "But without faith, it is impossible to please Him, for he who comes to God must believe that He exists and that He rewards those who diligently seek Him" *(Heb. 11:6).*

Hope

My vision is twofold; firstly, it is to reach the unreached, and secondly, it is to give hope to the hopeless in this hurting world. Does it look hopeless in your life? Let me encourage you that there is hope for you in Jesus Christ. When was the last time you faced a situation that seemed absolutely hopeless? Last week? Last month? Last year? This morning? Let me assure you that there is hope for all who feel hopeless. Please, believe this!

In Jesus Christ there is hope for you because with Him there is no situation that is hopeless. In Christ, God has given us a great deal to rejoice about. He had transformed my life from a death end into a highway of hope. Today in my life, whenever things look bad, I smile and rejoice because I know that in Christ no situation is hopeless, "For with God, nothing will be impossible" *(Luke 1:37)*. Before I gave my life to Jesus Christ, I used to make many endless plans that did not work. I wanted to do many things, only to be blocked by uncontrollable circumstances. I did not understand what was wrong with me. My problem was sin and unbelief.

Today I rejoice in the Lord because my redeemer lives. He overcomes all such limitations and conquered death on my behalf. He works for my good; my plans are blessed. His wonderful presence follows me in my life. "But the plans of the Lord stand forever, the purposes of His heart through all generations" *(Psalms 33:11)*.

My prayer for you is: "Now may the God of Hope fill you with all joy and peace in believing so that you may abound in hope by the power of the Holy Spirit" *(Romans 15:13)*. That is why I have said in my life that "I will hope in Christ, and I won't quit!" There is no man who is hopeless who puts his faith in Christ. At all times, I will put my trust in Christ whenever problems seem like too much for me, for I can handle them by faith.

Love

Naturally to me, sin was a way of life. I was living in total darkness in this crooked and perishing generation. But before I was lost forever, God's love arrested me. Before I was saved and consecrated in the love of God, I understood love as a feeling between me and my girlfriend, Nelly. But, oh! No. God's love is different from earthly love because it is unconditional with no strings attached. It is called AGAPE love. The world today is striving for this love.

Can you define that word? What is love? Love is a warm feeling of great friendliness. You have a pleasant time when you think of somebody else more than yourself. It is probably impossible to write a perfect definition of love. However, I keep on saying that love is a choice to give to others without expecting anything in return. That's the kind of love Jesus has for us, and that is the kind of love He wants us to demonstrate to others. Love is a choice. Love is as strong as death.

When God comes into our lives by faith, He calls us to make a choice and then enables us to live by the choice we made. Have you chosen the choice of love? "And now these three remain: faith, hope, and love; but the greatest of these is love" *(1 Cor. 13:13).*

As Christians, sometimes we do some good things to others but with selfish motives. We may do a favor for someone while deep inside we really hope for something in return.

CHAPTER TEN
WE ARE ON THE RUN

IN THE BEGINNING, GOD created the Heaven and the Earth. So, God created man in his own image. The Bible says, "This only have I found, that God hath made man upright, but they have sought out many inventions" *(Ecc. 7:29)*. Then the Devil deceived Eve into thinking that God was withholding something good from her and Adam and promised her that she would become a god.

After the fall of Adam and Eve into sin, they tried to cover themselves with fig leaves; they thought that they were making themselves acceptable to God. In the world today, man has tried many scientific inventions – "fig leaves" – which he uses as coverings for his sins, without depending on his creator.

Man's heart is a workshop of inventing various types of evils thinking that they will satisfy his heart's longing. Today in the heart of man, of whatever race and station in life, there is a hidden thirst for something he does not have (trace your part in this). Without the power of God controlling man's life, there are uncontrolled longings in the secret chambers of his heart. Although man is trying hard to satisfy himself by the present scientific achievements, it's all in vain.

Since the fall of Adam and Eve into sin, the Devil has been controlling man's life, corrupting the youth and the old. And man's heart is the source of sin. Jesus said, "For from within, out of the heart of man, proceedeth evil thought: adulteries, fornication, murders, thefts, conversions, an evil eye, blasphemy, pride, foolishness. All these things cometh from within and defile the man" *(Mark 7:20-23)*. Countless numbers of people today are deceived by the Devil; they find lies sweet. The Devil is leading man in the wrong truck of destruction; where there will be wailing and gnashing of teeth (Matthew 7:13). Yes, we are on the run, but where are we running to?

Surely money is increasing rapidly to some of us, but it has failed to bring peace in our societies and families. The more we have it, the more we become hard-hearted, proud, and envious. Money has left many of us thinking that we can rule the world with it. Some of us believe that money is the light of the world. But the Bible says, "The love of money is the root of all evil" *(1 Timothy 6:10)*. Everyone wants all the money in this world. Because of the love of money, you can hear of bank robberies, murder, and coup d'état to overthrow governments; these make up the evidence of man's greed for money.

The world is boiling with wars, each one fighting to be the master of others; desiring to keep them under bondage or exploit them. Although most of us would like to be happy and peaceful with what we have, the end result is the opposite. On the other hand, knowledge has also multiplied many times. Everyone is fighting to be self-sufficient with plenty of knowledge.

Many think that they are progressing, yet destruction is marching fast ahead of them. Without God, we'd be unable to live together. We'd hate each other; too much racial discrimination. Yes, knowledge has increased, but it is becoming poison to both man and animals. Through knowledge, man can now destroy the world in a split second.

Man's heart has become the workshop for discerning all kinds of evils in the world. Without Jesus, man will never be satisfied in this world. The world today is burning in sins and the smoke of sin goes up into Heaven before God. This is the reason why the word of God says, "O,' my God, I'm ashamed and blush to lift up my face to thee, my God, for our iniquities are increased over our head and our trespass is grown up unto the heavens" *(Ezra 9:6).* The world stands between life and death. Man's race for a better world has not yet succeeded.

The world is in the hands of a demon-inspired people who seem to drag down the world to degradation and domination. This is the sign of a crooked generation and the fulfillment of end-time prophecies. It is evident that something important is missing in the life of mankind. We are living in a most mysterious universe.

About this final race, the prophet, Amos, said, "Behold the days come, saith the Lord God, that I will send a famine into the land; not a famine of bread, nor thirst for water, but of hearing the words of the Lord. And they shall wander from sea to sea, and from north, even to the east. They shall run to-and-fro to seek the word of the Lord and not find it. In that day shall the fair virgins and young men faint for thirst" *(Amos 8:11-1).* This is the prophetic time when man is trying to get pure water when he has an impure fountain. Although man has tried to invent many things, he has failed to satisfy his inner longings.

Today in international meetings, the main agenda is peace; whereby the conveners talk about peace strategies. But if God could allow you to see the inside of their hearts, you'd see that they are actually planning war. The Word of God reveals man's problems. "The words of his mouth were smoother than butter, but war was in his heart: his words were softer than oil, yet were they drawn swords" *(Psalms 55:21)*. Man therefore can talk about peace, yet his heart, which should be the source of it, is very far from peace. "'There is no peace,' saith the Lord unto the wicked" *(Isaiah 48:22)*.

I believe that if the world could join together in faith and receive the Prince of Peace, Jesus Christ, the world would soon be at peace. The Bible says, "Therefore, being justified by faith, we have peace with God through our Lord Jesus Christ" *(Romans 5:1)*.

Many people are in bondage of evil powers in their souls and bodies. They cry for freedom, but they don't know the way of peace. Your heart and mind are the sources of all evils in the world today. "Your heart alone is deceitful above all things" *(Jeremiah 17:9)*. When Jesus Christ came here on Earth, He purposed to do the will of God, which is to give eternal life to mankind. "Jesus said unto them, 'I'm the bread of life, for he who cometh to me shall not hunger, and he who believeth in me shall never thirst'" *(John 6:40)*.

God is to show you the right path of life, for in His presence, there is fullness of joy. God loves you very much, so He has given you a wonderful invitation: "Ho, everyone who thirsteth, come to the waters, he who hath no money, come ye, buy, and eat; ye, come, buy wine and milk without money and without price; wherefore do ye spend money for that which is not bread? Hearken diligently unto me, eat ye that which is good, and let your soul delight itself in fattness. Incline your ear, come unto me and hear, and your soul shall live" *(Isaiah 55:1-3)*.

My friend, without Jesus Christ, there is no satisfaction in life. He is the bread and the water of life. It is God's design that the longings of the human heart shall be led to the one who is able to satisfy it. "For He satisfieth the longing soul and filleth the hungry soul with goodness" (Psalms 107:9) so that all men shall praise the Lord for His goodness, for it was the good pleasure of the Father that in Jesus shall all the fullness of God dwell. Jesus alone is the solution for this age.

CHAPTER ELEVEN
RUN TO JESUS

AS USUAL, IT WAS A mouth of blazing sunshine in the Kiambogo village because of climate change. It was the beginning of the year 1980 and, for a period of time, the rains had ceased. Everybody, including children, were busy preparing their farms to be ready for the next sowing season. The heat shimmered over the fields; a haze enveloped the distant hill. The sun had proceeded fast, baking the naked earth and making it too hot to work on. Men and women walked many miles to search for water. You could see them with their cattle knee-deep in the pond, swishing their tails lazily; and even the sheep seemed to be afflicted with severe heat and boredom. The area chief made many public notices warning people not to burn anything around, but nobody seemed to care. Oftentimes, people never learn from their mistakes.

Suddenly, under the red rays of light in the cloudless night, I opened my cottage door to go out, and to my surprise, I paused hundreds of times before I could get out. The night was red in the most horrible situation. The impetuous wind rattled fast, blowing the cedars up and down in the forest. The strong fire was now coming rapidly towards our house. The whole village was surrounded by red rays of light that could be seen very high in the air. The sound of fire and the falling trees could be heard some kilometers away. At a distance you could hear loud cries and shouts from children and women.

I stood trembling, looking at the scene, wondering, *who caused the fire? This is awful.* I abased myself in this sudden overcoming night of terror with impassive solemnity; I went in my house and made an altar beside my bed. I knelt down helplessly with no clothes and made a heavenly call. After prayers, I opened the door and felt very nervous. "Oh, God!" I cried in surprise.

My brother was asleep, but suddenly he was awakened by the shouts. He heard me crossing outside. He thought he was dreaming. Looking out through the open door, he saw with terror the village engulfed in fire. He was surprised; he had a vague sense of disquietude. It was as though he had been visited by a nightmare. The red light, which was fanned by the wind, was high in the air. To him it seemed unreal.

My younger brother was not saved yet, so he had some difficulties in seeing which way to turn for help. To him things were serious because death hanged on his shoulders. He joined me out in excitement. He saw the scene well and heard the screams from afar. When we saw a group of men marching together towards the scene, we went to join them.

The flames were strong because of the wind. The fire had a terrible noise like that of a railway engine at full speed. Everybody was puzzled. Someone commented, "Oh, dear! It's the end of the world!" Women kept screaming, and those who were asleep arose instantly as if by magic. "It is the end of the world!" several people repeated. The young children were helpless, so they enjoyed the scene just like a You could hear the roar of women screaming and many people walking and joining in excitement.

The old were too scared that their lives would soon collapse. They hobbled together, their eyes milky with age. Many of them were dried up and wrinkled in their faces, and their skin crinkled in folds on their bellies. They were tightened by cold and helplessly sitting together in a group waiting for death. They clung their lives to the young men who tried to rescue their lives. They all looked on at the scene as the young men struggled to stop the fire.

The old dug the ground with their long nails to get enough soil, which was used to stop the fire. They had forgotten everything they had in life. Some held branches in their withered hands and tried to help. People came from all corners, and they were very many like herds of gazelles in the Masai Mara Game Reserve. Suddenly, a bright light bathed them all, shining like silver on their faces and loose teeth. The light came from the head lumps of a big lorry. It came in speed and stopped in front of them. The lorry was carrying forest guards. Swiftly the driver cut off the engine and those on board howled and fell as they jumped down. You could hear their feet on the ground with a terrible sound as they were going toward the scene.

The first house was caught by flames of fire, which passed in speed. Some people ran fast for safety, as the whole village was a swell of fire. Here fire, there fire, and everywhere fire. The women swayed, packed together behind their folks, and sent out loud cries while their mates mingled in a fierce effort. Soon the men began to show their bravery by leaping into the air and spinning like traditional dancers. One woman clenched her thin hand and shouted, "Are you men or women?!" And the men answered boldly, "We are men!" The women wanted to stir the men.

Watching the heaving, stamping men was an old woman; she covered herself with a colored blanket and tightened herself in fear of cold. She saw the flashing of fire in speed. She heard the clatter of the flames like a machine gun. She also watched the fire as it zigzagged and bounced.

The forest guards used tactics to stop the fire, for they wanted to trace the course of this fire. In the morning, one could see properly the mob in the state where it had sacrificed itself the whole night. They all tried hard to put out the fire, but all was in vain. By noon, the fire had gained momentum due to the heat of the sun. Everybody was now busy fighting the fire.

Unfortunately, three people who were trying hard to put out the fire in the valley were suddenly caught unawares by the fierce red flames, which came in speed flying over them. "Look there!" somebody shouted. Soon you could hear loud cries in the valley below. These victims swayed on fire and shook their heads in roar and soon in drowning voices.

One man among them escaped; he came rolling from the tall grass, his body sweating and smelling of smoke. He was afraid; his fear caused him to regret having forsaken the others who died. With sweat pouring from his body, his heart was burning with shame. The others were burnt until nothing was left of them but a flame of bones.

Soon these victims' bodies were carried to the top. Many people came to see the bodies of these victims. Everybody felt sweat breaking in his or her body as they saw these victims. A woman began wailing after seeing the dead bodies until her husband caught her and said, "Enough." A young girl saw the bodies and fell down flat on the ground. Another woman saw the bodies and shouted, "Oh, God!" She began threshing her legs about because of fear.

A lad was almost beaten for asking for water in this time of danger. He was ordered to be silent and stand like a man. He cried with exhaustion, refusing to stand like a man in this time of danger. Everybody was shocked to see these victims who were burnt to death with no place of safety.

Truly I must say that this was the most horrible sight I have ever seen in my life. People being burnt until nothing is left of them but smoldering bones. It is terrible. Soon I heard a voice in my heart, which said, "My judgment is soon approaching this crooked generation." I can still remember the sorrow that was with the families of these victims; though they refused to be consoled because they knew that their loved ones were no more. When these people were buried, everything was thus backing to normal after this unusual episode in my village.

My friend, if death comes to you suddenly like those poor victims, where could you spend eternity? There is nowhere in this world in which you can find peace and safety for your soul. The world is in flames everywhere, making havoc of the economy. I know that you may have many ideas that will keep you moving in this life, but you will never make it. Many people today find life to be very boring due to inflation, but why worry? You will either die or live.

If you live, there is nothing to worry about; repent off your sins and come to Jesus. If you die in your sins, you'd think there would be nothing else to worry about; only to be prepared to join the Devil in Hell, where there will be wailing and gnashing of teeth forever. Are you feeling guilty for your sins? Don't resist; please, repent. I know one time you will remember all the evil things you have done before God. You will stand alone before God in the judgment seat.

Look at the marks of Jesus Christ. The ones He received for your sins. Lay every burden down to Him by faith and you will be a victor in this world. Jesus loves you, and even when life is hard or boring, He is always there to bless you. Jesus is the only way to make your life better now and forever.

You might have nothing to do with God in this life, but the day is approaching when you will die and stand before God. That day, your unbelief will disappear, and you will see God and His Son, Jesus, face to face. God does not want you to die before you repent. The Bible says, "'For I have no pleasure in the death of him who dieth,' saith the Lord God. 'Wherefore turn yourselves and live ye'" *(Eze. 18:32)*.

God does not like the death of a sinner, but the righteous will He preserve. If you repent now, you will not die the second death but live forever. The day is coming when everything will be open before your eyes and you will be prepared to receive your reward. "The wage of sin is death" *(Romans 6:25)*. The second death. The day of your salvation is now. "For when they shall say, 'peace and safety,' then sudden destruction cometh" *(1 Thess. 5:3)*.

Jesus is coming soon! Why don't you receive Him in your heart today? The decision is yours alone. God bless you. I think this story will help you to make a positive decision in your life now. The Fire Fell Suddenly. The fire fell over the plains of Sodom and Gomorrah. The people had wondered how it was possible for Lot's prophecy to be fulfilled. "Fire from Heaven

Fell." They laughed, but they did not know about the lake of fire beneath their feet; the large accumulation of gas and the heavy deposits of salt and Sulphur, which was to explode very high up in the air and drench them with the fury of the outraged almighty God.

In ignorance and unbelief, they thought it could not happen and concluded that Lot was mentally disturbed. The world never learns from its mistakes, and the majority still mock at the warning of God against their wickedness. They even think His prophets are fools or crazy.

The people of Sodom were proud, for they had enough bread, and their abundance of idleness expressed their standard of living. They produced such sexual depravity and homosexuality that in those days it was very unsafe to invite visitors to their homes. The people of Sodom were feeling secure in their orgies of self-indulgence. And suddenly the fire fell in the fearful flood over all that scene of iniquity. The only immediate warning they received was the hasty retreat of Lot and his family. Sudden terror took a hold of them. The majority had proved themselves fools. It had happened and is going to happen again soon.

"An example unto those who should afterwards live ungodly" *(2 Peter 2:6)*. Salvation was for the few, and destruction to the masses came in one short moment. "Likewise also as it was in the days of Lot. The same day that Lot went out of Sodom it rained fire and brimstone from Heaven and destroyed them all. Even thus shall it be in the day when the Son of Man is revealed" *(Luke 17:28)*. Suddenly this world will end by God, who is a consuming fire (Heb. 12:29).

The Holy God of Sinai, whose voice once shook the Earth when He gave laws to mankind, will once again shake not only the Earth but even the Heavens, too. When He calls all nations from the rising of the sun to the going down thereof; to appear for judgment. "'For behold, the day cometh that shall burn as an oven, and all the proud, yea, and all that do wickedly shall be stubble; and the day that cometh shall burn them up,' saith the LORD of hosts, 'that it shall leave them neither root nor branch'" *(Mal. 4:1).*

Our God shall come and shall not keep silence; a fire shall devour before Him, and it shall be very tempestuous around Him when He calls all mankind to give account. Since judgment must begin at the house of God— judgment according to light and understanding – He'll first call all those who have made a covenant with Him by sacrifice; those who made professing faith in the lamb of God that taketh away the sins of the world. "And if the righteous scarcely be saved, where shall the ungodly and the sinner appear?" *(1 Peter 4:18).*

No one should be uninformed with any doubt as to how this visible world will end while the timing of the event is God's secret. The Creator has described for us the world's destruction as clearly as language can be. "The day of the Lord will come as a thief in the night in which the Heavens shall pass away with great noise and the elements shall melt with fervent heat; the Earth also, and the works that are therein be burned up" *(2 Peter 4:18).*

From this vivid picture you should note these things. That destruction will be as unexpected as a thief in the night. The destruction will begin in the Heavens with great noise. When all planets, visible and invisible, will have caught fire, and the

Earth with its works will be burnt up. There will be nothing of this world but cosmic dust. I'm sure that no man made shelters or air-raid precautions will provide any protection from the fire of divine wrath. This world will be utterly destroyed and will not be reconditioned for further use. God will never give in because He is not a man. He cannot even retreat (Num. 23:19).

Suddenly The Rain Fell. Suddenly the rain fell for probably the first time in human history. Before this, God had sent forth his servant, Noah, to that generation, but they didn't seem to care. Now the rain fell just as the old eccentric Noah had been prophesying for years. How they had laughed at his predictions and mocked the building of the ark, which he said was ordained and designed by God Himself. They all laughed, and the jeer froze on their faces.

The rain fell, and the first drops of the prophesied flood fell onto their unturned faces. They looked hurriedly towards the ark into which Noah and his relatives had just retreated. The door was shut. As Noah had warned them, it was in God's hands, and they all knew that the door would be closed forever. Panic gripped the hearts of those people; terror such as they had never known crazed their minds because they never knew that this really was God's judgment, and they had been invited into the ark for safety.

But they had treated it all with scorn and contempt, and now the time of reckoning had come. It had happened. The door of mercy had been open for a long time, and now it was quickly closed; and immediately the floods came. The moment the obedient ones were in safety; the judgment fell onto the disobedient. No time elapsed between events. Salvation to the few and damnation to the wicked. Majority came in one short hour.

Compare this with, "AS IT WAS IN THE DAYS OF NOAH, SO SHALL IT BE ALSO IN THE DAYS OF THE SON OF MAN" *(Luke 17:26)*. When our Lord comes, He will weigh every man's virtues and crimes with undivided attention and a righteous scale. He will dispatch the workers of evil to Hell and usher the doers of righteousness into His Kingdom. I therefore plant my foot upon this ground of trust and silence every man's fear with "God is just." To the needy, He is merciful. Some will say, "Pardon me, O' Lord. Time has been very short." Yet I wonder who directs the Creator on His plans.

My creed is that the Lord saves whoever repents now. I believe that I will go to Heaven by faith and take my seat close to Jesus. This truth lays somewhere in the book of God. And this truth builds my faith most. My heart is filled with great love, and I'm elated to act after my call, for Jesus is coming soon to take me home. "What a wonderful day it must be when the sounds of a trumpet will be heard by the righteous only" *(1 Thes. 4:1)*. Wouldn't it be the greatest disaster for you to die in wickedness and eventually end up in Hell? Running to JESUS is escaping from Hell. Missing Heaven would be your greatest disaster for eternity.

About Us

Gospel Messengers Church is a nonprofit dedicated to transforming lives in Kenya's most marginalized communities. Committed to eradicating female genital mutilation (FGM), poverty, and illiteracy, the organization builds schools, provides clean water through boreholes, and empowers communities through education and sustainable development.

By addressing social injustices and uplifting vulnerable populations, Gospel Messengers Church fosters hope and opportunity for the less fortunate.

You can Donate via M-Pesa Pay Bill no: 880100 a/c: 5146870014.

You can also use PayPal email: messengergospel13@gmail.com

THESE ARE OUR BANK DETAILS FOR INTERNATIONAL MONEY TRANSFERS.

Bank Name	NCBA BANK KENYA PLC
Branch Name	NAKURU
Branch Code	000 (for any branch)
Bank Full Address	P.O. BOX 44599–00100, NAIROBI – KENYA
Bank Account Name	GOSPEL MESSENGER CHURCH
Bank Code	07
Bank Account Number	5146870014
SWIFT /BIC Code	CBAFKENX

Also by Peter N Muya

Kill Me Not
Love Without Lust
Do Not Weep
Death From Illicit Brew
Hope For Survival
I Shall Not Die
Never Lose Hope

Watch for more at https://www.gospelmessengerschurch.com.

www.ingramcontent.com/pod-product-compliance
Lightning Source LLC
Chambersburg PA
CBHW071334150726

47997CB00002B/718